VEGETARIAN COOKING FOR TWO

80 Perfectly Portioned Recipes for Healthy Eating

vegetarian
COOKING
FOR TWO

JUSTIN FOX BURKS AND AMY LAWRENCE

ROCKRIDGE
PRESS

Interior and Cover Designer: Elizabeth Zuhl
Art Producer: Meg Baggott
Editor: Justin Hartung

Cover photography by Hélène Dujardin. Food styling by Anna Hampton; Evi Abeler, ii, 129, 130; Hélène Dujardin, vi, 59; Marija Vidal, viii; Sarka Babicka/StockFood USA, x; Lilia Jankowska/StockFood USA, 16; Darren Muir, 35, 112; News Life Media/StockFood USA, 36; Bauer Syndication/StockFood USA, 60, 111; Jennifer Chong, 81; Roulier/Turiot/PhotoCuisine/StockFood USA, 82
Author photo courtesy of Justin Fox Burks Photo Studio

ISBN: Print 978-1-64876-908-5 | eBook 978-1-64876-909-2
R0

To all of you who
fell in love
with cooking
this past year.

contents

introduction

Hey there! It's Justin Fox Burks and Amy Lawrence, authors of three vegetarian cookbooks plus this one you're holding in your hands. We've tailored this book just for you. You see, we're not just cookbook authors but also a married couple. At home, it's just the two of us and our two pups. We've been together for more than 20 years and cook vegetarian meals at home every day. We know what you need because we live it.

If you're new to vegetarian cooking or you're looking to add some fantastic, out-of-the-box ideas to your meal rotation, this book is loaded with perfectly portioned vegetarian recipes for two. Whether you're a couple like us or you're newlyweds, empty nesters, or even roommates sharing cooking duties, this book will make cooking for your household a pleasure. In the past, you might have found many cookbook recipe yields to be outrageous for your needs, and we are here to help.

We achieved the goal of smaller-yield recipes by focusing each meal around fewer ingredients. That means less prep, fewer hours spent shopping and in the kitchen, fewer dishes in the sink, and more time for other pursuits. We want cooking to be a joy, not a chore. We even have a few recipes that don't require any cooking as well as guidance about some prepared ingredients that will save you time.

We really have no doubt that the recipes you choose to make from this book will become weeknight staples and weekend favorites. This goes for experienced cooks as well as kitchen novices. We'll walk you through the steps so that you end up with a delicious vegetarian dish every time.

Crêpes
with
Mint-and-
Pea Pesto
PAGE 34

chapter 1

EATING VEGETARIAN TOGETHER

The moment is here—it's time to get excited about vegetables! At its core, going vegetarian or just working more vegetarian meals into your life isn't about giving up anything—it actually opens up a new world of culinary possibilities.

When you're at the grocery store, spend a little more time in the produce department like we do, and dream up new ways to present something fresh and delicious. Make barbecue from that, stuff this into a taco shell, tuck those into a casserole. Don't worry, we've done a good bit of the imagining for you in this book, but these recipes can help fuel a new, creative way to think about fruits and vegetables. This book will help you focus your grocery list and end up with more complete meals and fewer leftover odds and ends. And we have ideas for any extra ingredients you have on hand, too.

A VEGGIE-FORWARD PLATE (OR TWO)

We all want to just snap our fingers and have a healthy, delish meal on the table that didn't take all night to prepare or drain our bank accounts. That's human nature. Preparing a meat-free meal really is conducive to these ends, and cooking for two helps focus on shopping for fewer ingredients for ease all around. You have to ask yourself, *Do I want to spend less money at the grocery store by cutting out expensive animal products?* (Of course you do!) *Would it benefit me to add more fresh vegetables to my diet?* (Yes, this can work wonders for one's health and well-being!) *Do I want to lower my blood pressure and maybe drop a few pounds?* (Who doesn't?)

Without promising anything monumental, studies have shown a link between a vegetarian diet and beneficial health outcomes. We've included popular dishes that we know are some of your favorites. You don't have to give up tacos, burritos, pizza, grilled cheese, pasta, or even burgers. You'll be putting all of those things on your table—just with a little twist. Here are five reasons a vegetarian diet is a great match for two-person cooking.

1. **Vegetarian pantry staples cost less and last longer.** Dried or canned beans, rice, and grains are all pennywise ways to fill your cupboard, your pot, and your plate. They keep for long periods of time and cut down on waste and trips to the store.

2. **Pairing pantry staples with fresh produce means you always have something on hand to cook.** Ripe avocado, sweet acorn squash, crisp lettuce, or a juicy summer tomato can bolster a meal and send it over the top. Appreciating these things and keeping select quantities on hand encourage you to cook fresh.

3. **Vegetarian meals are less expensive.** Although plant-based meats can cost as much as their real counterparts, our approach will save you money. We show you that cooking from the produce section, bulk bin, and canned goods aisle can help you spend less by creating appealing dishes out of staples.

4. **Protein is everywhere.** Fill your shopping cart with lentils, nuts, and leafy greens. Take a look: you've suddenly got a basket that's full of protein. Most people think of meat and dairy as the only sources of protein. But everything that grows has protein! And some vegetarian ingredients, like nuts and tofu, contain an especially high concentration of protein.

5. **Good vegetarian ingredients don't all need to be made from scratch.** Wrap something in a tortilla, and it becomes a meal. Don't fret about making the tortillas if that's intimidating right now. Perfectly good tortillas, bread, tomato sauce, and the like are available for decent prices at the grocery store. The same goes for condiments and spices. Soy sauce, curry powder, and sriracha can all be a joy to make yourself, but there is an excellent array of choices on the shelves. Take advantage of these products and stay nimble in the kitchen.

VEGETARIAN MEALS THAT SATISFY

The recipes in this book are designed to be filling and satisfying. We love to eat and to share a meal; our recipes reflect that. The following elements have been taken into consideration so that it's easy love this new way of cooking and eating.

All about Balance

Once upon a time, vegetarian food was just the same meal with the meat left off. It was a dark time for those of us who had to live through it. We remember those days and never plan to return, so we stack vegetables high and season with abandon. In this book, you'll find vegetables playing all the traditional roles in the starch-protein-vegetable triad that many meals rely on to be satisfying, keep you full, and provide you with energy. The difference is that we treat certain vegetables like other cooks would treat the protein and then highlight it at the center of the plate.

We use sweet potatoes, corn grits, pasta, rice, and bread for the foundation of many meals. These minimally processed starches give you a long, slow energy burn. Fresh vegetables, like broccoli, red peppers, winter squash, and cabbage, provide nutritional density to your meals. Beans and nuts contain lots of protein and will keep you full.

PLANT-POWERED BENEFITS

We all know that we should be eating more vegetables and less meat, but it's important to remember why. The American Heart Association asserts that the benefits are clear. So if you want to reduce your like-lihood of type 2 diabetes, obesity, stroke, heart disease, high blood pressure, cholesterol, and some types of cancer, then make it a goal to eat less meat. It's that simple: a healthy body can give you more energy to do all the things you love. Here are the ways a plant-powered diet can help you.

HEALTHY HEART: The American Heart Association explains that animal protein and full-fat dairy are responsible for much of the cholesterol-raising saturated fats that clog arteries, raise blood pressure, and increase the risk of a heart attack. So replacing those foods, or even just some of them, with vegetables can impact your heart health in positive ways.

HEALTHY WEIGHT: The Mayo Clinic describes people who follow a vegetarian diet as "generally leaner." Eating a vegetarian diet isn't an automatic ticket to weight loss, but it's a good start if you replace the meat you were eating with fruits and vegetables.

IMPROVES ENERGY: The *British Journal of Health Psychology* con-ducted a study of 300 people. The participants who kept a food diary reported that they felt more energetic the day they increased their intake of produce and also the following day. They also reported feeling calmer and happier when they ate more fruits and vegetables.

DECREASES RISK OF DIABETES: The National Institutes of Health assert that becoming a lifelong vegetarian decreases the risk of type 2 diabetes by 74 percent. That's significant! This is because nearly all type 2 diabetes cases are linked to lifestyle and diet. In one study, many participants with type 2 diabetes were able to reduce their insulin intake after starting a vegetarian diet.

SAVES YOU MONEY: Steak averages around $8 a pound versus tofu at $2 a pound. Now maybe you think that's not a fair comparison, but tofu actually has more protein per serving than beef does, according to Livestrong.com—so, the beans have it. There it is: more fiber, more protein, and more value.

EASILY ADAPTABLE: There are so many special diets these days, and vegetarian meals are easy to tweak to be Paleo, gluten-free, or vegan. Everyone can feel included at your table, and everyone can feel comfortable sitting down to roughly the same meal.

REWARDS CREATIVITY: Once you get in the habit of buying more vegetables and stocking up your pantry, there are so many preparations and combinations to try. Breaking out of the animal-protein-and-two-side-dishes routine can be surprisingly liberating.

For example, we use beans as burgers and portobellos as the filling in a French dip, roles traditionally reserved for meat. Smoked almonds make for a fantastic stand-in for bacon, and walnuts, almonds, and pine nuts are a welcome addition to any meal. We do use eggs and cheese in this book, so if you are craving non-vegetable-based protein, we give you some flexibility and a few options.

And don't worry, you'll get plenty of protein if you eat a variety of vegetables and even more if you partake in dairy and eggs.

Rethink Traditional

You won't miss a thing, we promise. In each chapter, we've included vegetarian and vegan takes on familiar classics, such as bagels and tomato "lox," chick'n sandwiches, Bolognese, tacos, pot pie, and lasagna. These are the dishes that we like to see on our table; maybe they're meals you have grown to love, too. We make these classics new by transforming them to be veg-forward and full of flavor. We employ simple, proven techniques that can take you from a vegetable novice to a vegetable pro.

Once you've mastered a few of these recipes, you'll be thinking of new ways to flip other old favorites to make them healthier, more vibrant, and even more appealing than the original.

Umami

What do seaweed, soy sauce, kimchi, shiitake mushrooms, garlic, and tomatoes all have in common? If you said "umami," you're right. So what is umami? Well, it's the fifth flavor sensation. It's last but not least. You have sweet, salty, sour, spicy . . . and umami. This is the flavor that many meat-based dishes have automatically, but vegetarian recipes can sometimes swing and miss. We concentrate on ingredients and cooking methods, like caramelizing and searing, that accentuate umami. We don't want you missing out on all that flavor, now do we?

Spice It Up

Think of flavor as a symphony and herbs and spices as each of the instruments. Lemon, salt, coriander, and vinegar hit the high notes, while black pepper, smoked paprika, and cumin hold the low end. In the middle are all the various fresh herbs giving us clues as to the timbre of the plate. Verdant basil can transport us to Italy with pesto or Thailand in a curry. Thyme often speaks to us in French, while parsley sings in multiple languages. Each spice, each flavor, each element makes a metaphorical sound, and we aim to create harmony on your plate.

Exploring Techniques

We have no shame in the kitchen. If a microwave is the best tool for the job, then we use a microwave. Why not? What we do in this book is use techniques that don't require a lot of special equipment. We won't have you run out and buy a sous vide machine or a spherification kit. We want dinner on the table in minimal time just like you do, but we won't compromise on flavor. That's why we zero in on the right technique for each dish. We coax out deep, rich flavors with a bake or a braise. We add a smoky tinge with the high heat of a cast-iron pan. You really can create all of this amazing flavor with vegetables!

SMART SHOPPING

Let's talk about the grocery store. It's a minefield of impulse shopping and over-buying. Go in with a plan. You're shopping for two, remember? Buy several small cans of tomatoes rather than a large can that will yield leftovers. Look to stock up on dry goods and plan out meals in advance that require fresh vegetables. Because there's nothing worse for a home cook than letting food go to waste.

Produce

You've probably heard that buying produce in season is best, and it's true! It's wonderful to incorporate what's currently growing into your diet and experience those amazing flavors. However, because many items are frozen when they are in season and at the peak of freshness, it makes sense to have frozen produce on hand, too. We always have bags of frozen green peas, berries, greens, sweet corn, edamame, veggie noodles, and tomato sauce in our freezer.

FIVE RECIPES TO TRY

We love matching a mood with a meal! Here are some suggestions that feature some of our favorite go-to recipes.

1   **IF IT'S A CLOUDY, LAZY MOVIE DAY:** When you just want to stay in your PJs and chill at home, a Big Burrito (page 48) will have you back on the couch and enjoying a filling meal in less than 15 minutes.

2   **IF YOU'RE HAVING DATE NIGHT AT HOME:** You bought the flowers, the candles are definitely getting lit, and you can't wait to catch up with your sweetie. Make Ginger-Peanut Cabbage Salad (page 46) and Sushi Bowls (page 88)—maybe along with a bottle of sake to share.

3   **IF IT'S A CHILLY DAY AND YOU NEED SOME COMFORT AND WARMTH:** Make Loaded Microwave Latkes (page 49), which are a meal all by themselves. We've made them easy and fun.

4   **IF YOU'RE RESISTING THE URGE TO ORDER TAKEOUT:** Have an Indian cuisine feast at home! Cook Chana Masala (page 70) for two for a comforting and vegan takeout fake-out.

5   **IF YOU'VE SPENT ALL OF YOUR TIME ON THE MAIN DISH AND NOW YOU NEED DESSERT FAST:** Whip up Date and Peanut Turtles (page 124)—they come together quickly with a little chopping and some microwaved dark chocolate.

Beans, Grains, and Dried Goods

Dry goods can make up an entire meal, so you'll never be without *something* to cook if you have a stocked pantry. Beans are essential. We keep our pantry stocked with inexpensive dried beans, but we also keep a few prepared cans of our favorites around just in case we need to whip up a quick plate of nachos. We keep nuts around for snacking and tossing into a salad or on top of a curry. Rice and pasta last forever and can be kept in the pantry. We buy these when they're on sale, and we aren't too picky about what kind or variety. We love them all.

Canned, Jarred, and Bottled Goods

Our refrigerator door is a gallery of pickled things, hot sauces of every stripe, mustards, ketchup, vegan mayonnaise, all manners of jam, and condiments from every country you can imagine. Luckily these things are small and last a while. Our pantry is more straightforward, with cans of beans, coconut milk, artichoke hearts, olives, and fire-roasted tomatoes; bottles of vinegar and olive oil; and jars of salsa, capers, and roasted red peppers. We often buy the smaller sizes of these items so half of the container doesn't languish in the refrigerator.

Dairy

One of us eats mostly vegan, so we swap in plant-based milks and cheeses pretty often. You can do this with any recipe we write. We use plant-based butter and cream cheese, and we honestly can't tell the difference. Since there's just two of us, we tend to buy single servings of items like yogurt and small packages of Cheddar, mozzarella, and blue cheese. Just be aware of how often you use these items, and make sure you get them into rotation before the expiration date.

MAKING THE MOST OF INGREDIENTS

We designed this book to have minimal extra ingredients and not many, if any, leftovers of the finished dishes. We've tailored each recipe to be just right for a smaller audience of two. To achieve this, shop for smaller cans, buy dry goods in bulk to procure just what you need, and seek the right size and number of fresh

BONUS BUDGETING

People often complain about how costly it is to be vegan or vegetarian. If you're buying $7 avocado toast rather than making your own, it *is* expensive. Cooking for yourself and the one you love at home can really stretch those bucks. We'd like to present a few other ways to do just that.

BUY IN BULK: The bulk aisle in the grocery store is a treasure trove of money savings. We buy nuts, rice, oats, grains, and dried fruit there. You're saving money because there's no marketing or packaging to pay for, so you totally win.

DON'T BUY ALL ORGANIC: Look for sales on organic produce and buy it when it seems reasonable, especially for items like strawberries and greens. There's no need to buy organic avocados or mushrooms. We often refer online to the lists concerning this topic.

COOK YOUR OWN BEANS: There are only 1½ cups of beans in a typical 15-ounce can. If you can plan ahead and soak your dried beans overnight before cooking them, you'll save about a dollar on each meal. That adds up quickly.

TRY A CSA BOX: This acronym stands for "community-supported agriculture." You get a good deal on locally produced goods, and the farmer knows that they are going to make a sale—a real win for everyone. Although you don't always get to choose what you get, the upside is that it's always fresh and in season.

KEEP YOUR EYES PEELED FOR A DEAL: Olive oil and coffee beans tend to bump up the price of our grocery hauls. We keep a close eye out for deals and comparison shop on these higher-dollar items. When it's feasible, we stock up.

ingredients. Will you have some leftovers here and there? Yes, that's inevitable. Here are some ideas that'll help you never waste a thing.

Use It Up

We offer guidance throughout the book on how to use up everything. We get creative with all kinds of ingredients, but we'd never leave you holding the half-empty bag. Each recipe chapter includes a "Use It Up" sidebar that suggests how to maximize ingredients. With a little planning and experience, you'll save money just by utilizing what you have. After all, food waste is a critical issue, and we all can do our part to keep food out of landfills.

For example, we include an idea about how to use maple syrup to sweeten an herbal lemonade, and Greek yogurt can be substituted anywhere you might use sour cream or, with a little sweetener, even whipped cream.

Storage Solutions

Knowing how to store your ingredients properly can help you make the most of them before they expire.

FRESH HERBS: Wash and dry herbs as soon as you pick them or get home and unpack them. Store them in an airtight container for up to a week. If you feel like you won't get around to using them, just make a pesto with olive oil and any nuts you have on hand and freeze it until you're ready to use it.

LETTUCE AND MIXED GREENS: Similar to fresh herbs, wash greens and dry them off right away. Store them loosely in a container lined with a dry paper towel.

MUSHROOMS: Mushrooms should be taken out of the container and placed into a paper bag—they tend to deteriorate quickly when their moisture is trapped.

ONIONS: Even if you don't need a whole onion, go ahead and dice the whole thing. Just place the unused portion in a small container and store it in the freezer for later use.

CHEESE: Wrap hard cheeses loosely in wax paper, and be sure to keep them in the cheese drawer if your refrigerator has one. This is humidity controlled and optimized for such ingredients.

TOMATOES: Store tomatoes outside of your refrigerator; the cold will make them mealy. They're so pretty that we just keep them out on the countertop in a decorative bowl. Store them stem-side down and they'll last longer.

BANANAS: We try to buy these in stages of ripeness, and we keep them in a fruit bowl on the countertop so we can monitor them and use them up accordingly: maybe some are browning and ready to be blended into smoothies, pancakes, or bread, and others are firm enough to be sliced and used on top of smoothie bowls or oatmeal.

TOOLS FOR TWO

You really won't need a bunch of special tools to make stellar meals for two. It's likely that you already have some basic tools, such as a cutting board, a good sharp knife, mixing bowls, wooden spoons, and silicone spatulas. Here are some other tools that can be helpful to add to your kitchen.

A 12-inch **cast-iron pan** can be found for around $20, and you will get a lifetime of use out of it. Use it to make taco fillings, pancakes, and corn bread and to roast anything and everything. That said, for most of the recipes in this book, you can always use a regular skillet or frying pan.

A **silicone brush** is the easiest way to coat a baking pan with butter or oil or to add a sauce to a dish before baking.

An extra-large **mixing bowl** will help you contain any potential mess! Truly, a mixing bowl can never be too big, but it certainly can be frustrating if it's too small.

An 8-inch **chef's knife** that fits your budget and feels comfortable in your hand will always be helpful in making quick work of chopping vegetables.

We also love inexpensive **ceramic knives** because they can go point-side down in the dishwasher. Having a few different sizes of these and at least one that's serrated can make life a lot easier in the kitchen.

A full-size **rimmed sheet pan** or jelly roll pan is great for roasting vegetables and making cookies.

Parchment paper is something you will use every week to line sheet pans and baking dishes.

MEAL PLANNING FOR A PAIR

One of the best ways you can use up ingredients and avoid leftovers is just by planning ahead. In developing the dishes for this book, we've made every effort to call for ingredients that can be used up completely in each of the recipes. However, being strategic with meal planning can still be helpful, especially when you can't buy a small amount of certain ingredients. What follows are some ideas for how to plan vegetarian meals for two.

Select meals that use similar ingredients. This is a nice way to keep from getting overwhelmed by shopping and cooking. You can always vary your recipes the next week and take advantage of new ingredients to highlight.

Stock up on pantry staples. Beans, grains, and the like are the basis for so many meals, and they sure do save you money and also keep for a long while.

Be judicious about the fresh ingredients you purchase. Buy what looks great and only what you already love if you are just starting out on your vegetarian cooking journey. You can always branch out and try a few different things once you grow more confident in your cooking skills.

The freezer is your friend. One of our pals who is a chef says that the answer is always "yes" if the question is "Can I freeze it?"

Buy vegetarian bouillon cubes. They take up little room in the cupboard and last for a very long time.

Be flexible. If you happen to have a different variety of, say, a bean or nut than a recipe calls for, have no qualms about swapping in what you already have on hand if it makes sense.

THE RECIPES IN THIS BOOK

The recipes in this book are designed to make satisfying vegetarian dishes for two adults without leftovers to deal with the next day. This gives you the freedom to try new things, learn what you especially like to cook and to eat, and quickly find your rhythm with vegetarian cooking. Here are a few more helpful labels and tips that we've included in each recipe chapter.

Cooking for, how shall we say, an *overly discerning* partner or house-mate can be tricky whether the meals you are creating are vegetarian or not. Here are some ideas for how to handle the situation—keep these tips in your back pocket, and you'll have a few ways to keep the peace at mealtimes.

Ask your partner for input about meals—and make an occasion out of cooking together. One person should never be doing all the shopping and cooking. That's a recipe for burnout. So put on some music, open some wine, and make the everyday task of cooking another facet of a strong relationship.

Swap in vegetables you know you both like. This is pretty important. Mealtimes encompass many things, from negotiation to collaboration, but they should never be a battle! Start with what you have in common and then build on what you like.

Choose flexible meals. If one person is into bread and the other is avoiding gluten, make sure the starchy element of the meal is an option rather than the main focus. For example, one person may want a burrito while the other prefers a burrito bowl, sans tortilla.

Compromise is key. Trying new things can be an adventure when you're both in it together. Maybe you thought you never liked mush-rooms, but a new preparation that uses spice and a small dice might change your mind. Likewise, when your partner craves asparagus and it's not your favorite, talk about ways that might make it more palatable and give it a shot.

Take the lead—and then jump in the passenger seat. Why not switch off leadership roles as you rotate through meals throughout the week? One person shops, the other cooks. Or offer to be the cleanup crew or the official vegetable chopper. Support each other and make it fun.

LABELS THAT INDICATE EASE: Many of our recipes fall into categories that highlight how easy they are: **One Pot** (or pan or bowl), **5-Ingredient** (not counting salt, pepper, olive oil, or water), **30 Minutes or Less,** and **Minimal Prep** (no more than 5 minutes). You will see a variety of these labels in each chapter's selection of recipes.

"USE IT UP" ADVICE: Although these recipes have been designed to deliver two perfect portions, there will be some instances when you have extra ingredients. In each chapter, we provide advice about what to do with some of those ingredients along with a mini recipe or two. For example, one of our favorite things to do with leftover rice is make a bowl of Breakfast Fried Rice (page 21), but we also suggest a delicious mango-and-honey rice dish that is an unexpected dessert. We also offer a surprising savory use for granola on a salad.

DESSERTS FOR TWO: Although nearly 90 percent of the recipes in this book are for meals, we've also included 10 recipes in our Desserts chapter. To be honest, homemade sweets really can present a challenge when you're cooking for two. We think novelty is better than quantity, and we designed these recipes to produce reasonable yields for two people to enjoy something sweet at the end of the meal. We've also provided some recipes for healthier desserts that are lower in sugar.

Yogurt, Citrus, and Granola Parfait
PAGE 33

chapter 2

BREAKFAST AND BRUNCH

Apple, Raisin, and Pecan Twirls

When we were young, we used to unroll our sweet rolls until they resembled sticky, cinnamon-y measuring tape. Now is your chance to turn back the clock and actually roll *up* some delicious baked goods instead. We start with pizza dough and add apples, raisins, and pecans for a pastry that's perfect for greeting the day. These twirls would also be a lovely dish to prepare for a holiday brunch or special Valentine's Day breakfast or as a treat on your anniversary.

PREP TIME: 30 MINUTES, PLUS 45 MINUTES TO RISE

COOK TIME: 40 MINUTES

SWAP IT:

Substitute pears and dried cranberries for the apples and raisins to enjoy a different flavor profile.

1 (7- to 9-ounce) package pizza dough
1¼ cups diced peeled apples
½ cup raisins
2 tablespoons unsalted butter
1 tablespoon brandy
Juice of ½ lemon
½ cup chopped pecans
¼ cup packed light brown sugar
½ teaspoon kosher salt

1. Remove the dough from the refrigerator. Place it on the counter for 30 minutes to make it easier to work with.
2. In a microwave-safe bowl, combine the apples, raisins, butter, brandy, and lemon juice. Microwave on high for 1 minute.
3. Add the pecans, sugar, and salt. Mix until evenly distributed.
4. Place the dough on a sheet of parchment paper, and using a rolling pin, roll into a roughly 9-by-12-inch rectangle.
5. Spread the mixture evenly over the dough, then roll up starting from a short side.
6. Line a sheet pan with parchment paper.

7. Cut the roll into 6 even pieces and place on the prepared sheet pan, cut-side up.
8. Cover with a dish towel and let rise for 45 minutes.
9. While the twirls are rising, preheat the oven to 350°F.
10. Transfer the sheet pan to the oven and bake for 40 minutes, or until the twirls are golden. Remove from the oven.

ADD IT:
Something sweet plus something savory is usually our plan for a hearty weekend brunch. Serve these twirls along with Tofu Scramble Extraordinaire (page 22) or Herbed Omelet (page 24) and a fresh fruit salad drizzled with honey and a pinch of cayenne pepper.

PER SERVING (1 TWIRL):
CALORIES: 292;
FAT: 12G; PROTEIN: 4G;
CARBOHYDRATES: 43G;
FIBER: 2G; SODIUM: 470MG

Grits Casserole

In the South, we call them grits, but you may have experienced them as polenta or corn mash. It's all the same stuff, really. We banish the usual practice of incessant stirring because in this recipe, the oven does all the work for you. The grits are creamy and flavorful—we know you'd expect nothing less!

ONE POT
MINIMAL PREP

PREP TIME: 5 MINUTES

COOK TIME: 50 MINUTES

PAIR IT:

This dish makes for an excellent accompaniment to Potato Hash (page 26).

PER SERVING:
CALORIES: 501;
FAT: 24G; PROTEIN: 25G;
CARBOHYDRATES: 45G;
FIBER: 3.5G; SODIUM: 793MG

½ cup quick-cooking yellow grits
1 (14½-ounce) can diced fire-roasted tomatoes
1½ cups water
½ cup shredded smoked Gouda
  or Cheddar cheese
1 teaspoon Cajun seasoning
½ cup sliced scallions, green and white parts
1 tablespoon olive oil
4 large eggs
Hot sauce, for garnish

1. Preheat the oven to 400°F.
2. In a medium (roughly 6-by-10-inch) casserole dish, combine the grits, tomatoes, water, cheese, Cajun seasoning, scallions, and oil until well mixed.
3. Crack the eggs, one at a time, into each quadrant of the dish. Cover with aluminum foil.
4. Transfer the dish to the oven and bake for 45 to 50 minutes, or until the whites have set. Remove from the oven.
5. Spoon the eggs and grits into 2 shallow bowls.
6. Garnish with hot sauce.

Breakfast Fried Rice

We love to find ways to eat actual vegetables for breakfast or brunch. Leftover rice and some odds and ends of vegetables are all you really need for our version of this classic dish. Use any vegetables you have in the refrigerator: broccoli, scallions, carrots, mushrooms . . . whatever! We finish it off with a fried egg on top, and it's amazing.

2 tablespoons toasted sesame oil or olive oil, divided
2 large eggs
2 cups finely chopped mixed vegetables
2 cups cold leftover rice
1 tablespoon soy sauce
1 teaspoon sriracha

1. Heat a large nonstick skillet or a wok over high heat. Pour in 1 tablespoon of oil.
2. Add the eggs. Cook for 5 minutes, or until very crispy on the bottom and the whites have set.
3. Working fast, remove the eggs and set aside, then add the remaining 1 tablespoon of oil and the vegetables. Cook, stirring or tossing every 30 seconds, for 3 to 4 minutes, or until their color deepens.
4. Add the rice and cook for 2 to 3 minutes. Remove from the heat.
5. Stir in the soy sauce and sriracha.
6. Divide the rice mixture between 2 plates.
7. Top each plate with a fried egg.

30 MINUTES OR LESS
ONE POT

PREP TIME: 15 MINUTES

COOK TIME: 15 MINUTES

USE IT UP:
Toasted sesame oil has a great pork-like flavor, and it's also used in Portobello Mushroom Bacon (page 25) and Black-Eyed Pea Sausages (page 29).

PER SERVING:
CALORIES: 511;
FAT: 20G; PROTEIN: 15G;
CARBOHYDRATES: 66G;
FIBER: 4.5G; SODIUM: 617MG

Tofu Scramble Extraordinaire

This is an update to a classic vegan dish we've been eating for decades. We've modernized it with some curry powder and crunchy vegetables. You may never make plain old scrambled eggs again. Be sure to add the tomatoes at the last minute so they keep their shape and flavor.

30 MINUTES OR LESS
ONE POT

PREP TIME: 10 MINUTES
COOK TIME: 10 MINUTES

SWAP IT:

Substitute 1 bunch trimmed asparagus for the bell pepper for a more refined version of this dish. If you're not eating eggs, opt for vegan mayonnaise.

PER SERVING:
CALORIES: 350;
FAT: 23G; PROTEIN: 23G;
CARBOHYDRATES: 16G;
FIBER: 7G; SODIUM: 628MG

1 tablespoon olive oil
1 small green bell pepper, diced
1 bunch scallions, sliced, green parts reserved for garnish
1 (14-ounce) package extra-firm tofu, drained and crumbled
1 tablespoon mayonnaise
1 tablespoon curry powder
1 teaspoon kosher salt
1 cup halved cherry tomatoes

1. Heat a large nonstick or cast-iron skillet over medium-high heat.
2. Pour in the oil and add the bell pepper and scallions. Sauté for 5 minutes.
3. Add the tofu, mayonnaise, curry powder, and salt. Cook for 5 minutes. Remove from the heat.
4. Stir in the tomatoes.
5. Serve the scramble garnished with the reserved green parts of the scallion.

Banana-Oat Smoothie Bowls

This healthy, hybrid breakfast combines superfood oats with potassium-packed bananas. It's the perfect way to perk up your morning routine, especially when the weather is warm. You'll never get tired of this because it's infinitely customizable. Just swap out the toppings to suit your mood, or use whatever you have on hand.

2 medium bananas, frozen
½ cup quick-cooking oats
1½ cups unsweetened whole regular or plant-based milk
1 tablespoon maple syrup
Juice of ½ lemon
¼ teaspoon ground cinnamon
⅛ teaspoon kosher salt
Dried and fresh fruit, seeds, nut butters, and honey, for garnish

1. In a blender, combine the bananas, oats, milk, maple syrup, lemon juice, cinnamon, and salt. Blend until mostly smooth.
2. Divide the mixture between 2 shallow bowls.
3. Garnish with dried and fresh fruit, seeds, nut butters, and honey.

30 MINUTES OR LESS
ONE POT
MINIMAL PREP

PREP TIME: 5 MINUTES

ADD IT:
Nut butter, such as almond, peanut, or cashew, is a terrific topper for this smoothie bowl.

PER SERVING (WITHOUT GARNISHES):
CALORIES: 346;
FAT: 8G; PROTEIN: 11G;
CARBOHYDRATES: 61G;
FIBER: 5.5G; SODIUM: 151MG

Herbed Omelet

Omelets are so simple but require some technique to get just right. Here we use a little kitchen hack to make it easy. The omelet is started on the stovetop and finished under the broiler so it cooks evenly, no flipping required. *Voila!*

**30 MINUTES
OR LESS**

MINIMAL PREP

PREP TIME: 5 MINUTES

COOK TIME: 5 MINUTES

USE IT UP:

Swiss cheese is something we like to have on hand in the refrigerator because not only is it wonderful in an omelet, but also it makes for an excellent grilled cheese sandwich or a topping for a roasted root vegetable side dish. In addition, we like to melt slices of it over baked spaghetti squash and marinara.

PER SERVING:
CALORIES: 311;
FAT: 24G; PROTEIN: 21G;
CARBOHYDRATES: 2G;
FIBER: 0.5G; SODIUM: 479MG

4 large eggs
2 scallions, sliced, green parts
reserved for garnish
3 thyme sprigs, stemmed
1 tablespoon chopped fresh parsley,
plus more for garnish
½ teaspoon kosher salt
½ teaspoon black pepper
1 tablespoon unsalted butter
2 slices Swiss cheese

1. In a large bowl, whip together the eggs, scallions, thyme, parsley, salt, and pepper until bubbles form on top of the mixture.
2. Set the broiler on high.
3. Heat a 10-inch oven-safe pan over high heat until wisps of smoke appear on the surface.
4. Put the butter in the pan, and as soon as it melts, add the egg mixture. Cook for 30 seconds on the stovetop, but do not move the eggs. Remove from the heat.
5. Place the pan under the broiler for 2 minutes, or until the eggs have set. Remove from the oven.
6. Top the omelet with the cheese, and using a spatula, fold in half.
7. Cut the omelet in half and place each half on a plate.
8. Garnish with the reserved green parts of the scallions and more parsley.

Portobello Mushroom Bacon

We often look at an ingredient and ask ourselves, "Can you make bacon out of that?" The answer is usually a resounding *yes*. Coconut, eggplant, potato skins, and almonds have all been subjected to this experiment. Among our favorites is the meaty texture of portobello mushrooms. We add sweet and savory flavors, bake them, and we're off to Breakfastland.

1 teaspoon smoked paprika
½ teaspoon black pepper
1 tablespoon maple syrup
1 tablespoon soy sauce
1 tablespoon toasted sesame oil
2 medium portobello mushrooms,
  cut into ⅛-inch-thick slices

1. Preheat the oven to 400°F. Line a sheet pan with parchment paper.
2. In a medium bowl, whisk together the paprika, pepper, maple syrup, soy sauce, and oil.
3. Arrange the mushroom slices cut-side down in a single layer on the prepared sheet pan.
4. Brush with the liquid mixture until it's all used up.
5. Transfer the sheet pan to the oven and bake for 25 minutes. Remove from the oven.

5-INGREDIENT

30 MINUTES OR LESS

MINIMAL PREP

PREP TIME: 5 MINUTES

COOK TIME: 25 MINUTES

SWAP IT:

Thinly slice a medium eggplant and use the same method to create eggplant bacon for sandwiches and salads.

PER SERVING:
CALORIES: 109;
FAT: 7.5G; PROTEIN: 2G;
CARBOHYDRATES: 10G;
FIBER: 1G; SODIUM: 448MG

Potato Hash

This recipe is something that you *need* to learn how to make, because it means you'll never have to buy frozen hash browns again. This breakfast and brunch classic pairs well with many of the other recipes in this chapter or even works as a healthier-than-French-fries side with a sandwich at lunchtime. The smoked paprika, one of our favorite spices, adds plenty of depth to this simple dish.

30 MINUTES OR LESS
ONE POT

PREP TIME: 15 MINUTES

COOK TIME: 10 MINUTES

SWAP IT:
Sweet potatoes make this dish a whole different experience. Give them a try!

PER SERVING:
CALORIES: 124;
FAT: 2.5G; PROTEIN: 3G;
CARBOHYDRATES: 24G;
FIBER: 3G; SODIUM: 288MG

1 tablespoon olive oil
1 medium russet potato, diced
1 small onion, diced
1 medium green bell pepper, diced
½ teaspoon smoked paprika
½ teaspoon kosher salt
¼ teaspoon black pepper
½ teaspoon apple cider vinegar

1. Heat a large skillet over medium-high heat.
2. Pour in the oil and add the potato. Cook for 5 minutes, or until the potato begins to brown on one side.
3. Stir in the onion and bell pepper. Cook for 5 minutes, or until the potatoes have cooked through.
4. Add the paprika, salt, pepper, and vinegar. Stir to coat. Remove from the heat. Serve warm.

Tomato Lox and Bagels

Roma tomatoes have just a few seeds and the most "meaty" flavor of any tomato variety. They're also pretty much available year-round at the grocery store. Our favorite thing to do with these little beauties is to thinly slice them and add a little sweet and savory spice mix the same way one might cure salmon to make lox. We pile the tomatoes high over toasted bagels with all the trimmings. No seafood needed!

2 medium Roma tomatoes, sliced
¼ teaspoon kosher salt
¼ teaspoon black pepper
¼ teaspoon sugar
¼ teaspoon chopped fresh dill
¼ teaspoon smoked paprika
2 bagels
4 to 8 tablespoons cream cheese, at room
   temperature
1 medium shallot, sliced
1 hardboiled egg, sliced
1½ teaspoons capers, drained

1. In a medium bowl, combine the tomatoes, salt, pepper, sugar, dill, and paprika. Toss to coat. Let rest for 5 minutes so that the flavors are infused.
2. While you wait, split and toast the bagels.
3. Spread the cream cheese on each bagel half.
4. Discard the liquid that has collected at the bottom of the bowl. Divide the marinated tomatoes among the 4 bagel halves.
5. Top with the shallot, egg, and capers.

30 MINUTES OR LESS

ONE POT

MINIMAL PREP

PREP TIME: 5 MINUTES

COOK TIME: 5 MINUTES

SWAP IT:

Skip the egg and use nondairy alternatives like Daiya or Tofutti brand cream cheese to make this breakfast dish vegan.

PER SERVING:
CALORIES: 506;
FAT: 19G; PROTEIN: 18G;
CARBOHYDRATES: 65G;
FIBER: 4G; SODIUM: 929MG

Peanut Butter and Banana-Stuffed French Toast

If you're looking for some warm comfort food that'll satisfy the kid in you, try this nostalgic recipe. These peanut butter and banana sandwiches are dipped in egg and given the French toast treatment.

PREP TIME: 10 MINUTES

COOK TIME: 25 MINUTES

SWAP IT:

Replace the banana and peanut butter with sliced apples and almond butter for a different take.

PER SERVING:
CALORIES: 610;
FAT: 29G; PROTEIN: 21G;
CARBOHYDRATES: 72G;
FIBER: 3G; SODIUM: 469MG

4 slices bread

¼ cup peanut butter

1 medium banana, sliced

½ cup whole milk

2 large eggs

2 teaspoons unsalted butter, divided

¼ cup maple syrup

1. Preheat the oven to 350°F.
2. Make 2 sandwiches using 2 slices of bread, half of the peanut butter, and half of the banana slices for each.
3. In a large mixing bowl, whisk together the milk and eggs.
4. Dip the sandwiches in the egg mixture, turning to coat, and let soak for 5 minutes.
5. Place 1 teaspoon of butter in the bottom of a medium casserole dish.
6. Place the sandwiches on top.
7. Add ½ teaspoon of butter to the top of each sandwich.
8. Transfer the casserole dish to the oven and bake for 25 minutes, or until the eggs have set. Remove from the oven.
9. Serve the French toast warm with the maple syrup.

Black-Eyed Pea Sausages

Oats are not just healthy and delicious. In this recipe, they act as a binder to hold the rest of the ingredients together. Shaped into patties and panfried, the oat mixture recreates the texture of traditional breakfast sausage.

1 (15-ounce) can black-eyed peas, drained and rinsed
1 cup quick-cooking oats
1 tablespoon toasted sesame oil
½ teaspoon dried sage
⅛ teaspoon ground nutmeg
⅛ teaspoon ground cloves
½ teaspoon kosher salt
1 tablespoon olive oil

1. In a large mixing bowl, combine the black-eyed peas, oats, sesame oil, sage, nutmeg, cloves, and salt. Using your hands or a potato masher, knead until a dough-like consistency forms. Set aside for 10 minutes to allow the moisture to distribute.
2. Using a ¼-cup measure, form the mixture into 8 patties, smoothing the edges so that the patties hold together better.
3. In a pan, heat the olive oil over medium heat.
4. Add the patties and panfry for 4 minutes per side, or until browned. Remove from the heat. Drain on paper towels and serve warm.

30 MINUTES OR LESS

PREP TIME: 15 MINUTES

COOK TIME: 10 MINUTES

PAIR IT:

Waffle Breakfast Sandwiches (page 30) are the perfect partner for these homemade vegetarian sausages.

PER SERVING (2 PATTIES):
CALORIES: 241;
FAT: 9G; PROTEIN: 8G;
CARBOHYDRATES: 32G;
FIBER: 6G; SODIUM: 448MG

Waffle Breakfast Sandwiches

Who says you can't have it all? Not us! This breakfast sandwich has a little bit of everything. Waffles: check; eggs: present; sausage: yes, ma'am; syrup: yup; cheese: why the heck not? The waffle indentations catch the good stuff, so all you have to do is pick this up and eat it like a sandwich. (We do recommend two napkins, though!)

5-INGREDIENT ONE POT

PREP TIME: 20 MINUTES

COOK TIME: 20 MINUTES

SMART SHOPPING:

Commercially available vegetarian breakfast sausage is a good stand-in when you just don't have a few extra minutes to make your own. We like sharp or extra-sharp Cheddar for this dish.

PER SERVING:
CALORIES: 695;
FAT: 37G; PROTEIN: 26G;
CARBOHYDRATES: 66G;
FIBER: 7.5G; SODIUM: 1,221MG

1 tablespoon olive oil
2 large eggs
4 frozen waffles
Kosher salt
Black pepper
1 teaspoon maple syrup
3 ounces Cheddar cheese, thinly sliced
4 Black-Eyed Pea Sausages (page 29)

1. Heat a medium nonstick skillet over medium heat.
2. Pour in the oil and crack the eggs into the skillet. Cook for 2 minutes.
3. Meanwhile, toast the waffles.
4. Flip the eggs and cook for 1 minute, or until the whites have set but the yolk is runny. Season with salt and pepper. Remove from the heat.
5. Divide the maple syrup and cheese between 2 of the toasted waffles.
6. Top each with 2 sausages, 1 over-easy egg, and another waffle.

Gluten-Free Fluffy Pancakes

We had lofty aspirations for these fluffy, airy pancakes. A little extra baking powder gives them a puff and a lift that'll make you feel like you're eating clouds in the morning.

1 cup gluten-free all-purpose flour
1 large egg
2 teaspoons baking powder
½ teaspoon kosher salt
1 cup whole milk
1 tablespoon unsalted butter

1. To make the batter, in a large mixing bowl, whisk together the flour, egg, baking powder, salt, and milk until smooth.
2. In a large cast-iron or nonstick skillet, melt the butter over medium heat.
3. Using a ¼-cup measure, spoon the batter onto the hot skillet. Cook for 2 to 3 minutes per side, or until very fluffy, cooked through, and golden brown. Remove from the heat.

5-INGREDIENT

30 MINUTES OR LESS

PREP TIME: 10 MINUTES

COOK TIME: 10 MINUTES

SWAP IT:

Use regular all-purpose flour if you're not interested in going the gluten-free route.

PER SERVING:
CALORIES: 400;
FAT: 13G; PROTEIN: 13G;
CARBOHYDRATES: 56G;
FIBER: 0G; SODIUM: 369MG

Our Favorite Avocado Toast

This is likely the recipe we make most often for breakfast. Honestly, Justin eats this dang near every morning, so that's quite an endorsement. It's easy to make even before you've had your coffee, and it offers an irresistible combination of savory, spicy, and crunchy. We like to use Campari tomatoes, but really any will do.

5-INGREDIENT

30 MINUTES OR LESS

ONE POT

PREP TIME: 10 MINUTES

SMART SHOPPING:

Buy avocados in threes: one that yields to gentle pressure and is ripe, one that is firmer, and one that's hard as a rock. They'll be ready to go at different times so you always have a good one on hand.

PER SERVING:
CALORIES: 260;
FAT: 17G; PROTEIN: 6G;
CARBOHYDRATES: 25G;
FIBER: 6G; SODIUM: 423MG

1 teaspoon sriracha
1 tablespoon regular or vegan mayonnaise
2 slices whole-grain bread, toasted
1 large ripe avocado, pitted, peeled, and sliced
2 small tomatoes, sliced
¼ teaspoon kosher salt
⅛ teaspoon black pepper

1. Spread the sriracha and mayonnaise on each toast slice.
2. Layer the avocado and tomatoes on each slice. Pile it high. Season with the salt and pepper.

Yogurt, Citrus, and Granola Parfait

This no-cook breakfast awakens the senses with citrus aromas and keeps you digging in for that crunchy granola. We top ours with chia and pomegranate seeds for an extra-healthy dose of good stuff first thing in the morning.

2 (5.3-ounce) containers plain Greek yogurt
1¼ cups granola
1 small grapefruit
2 medium oranges
1 small apple, cored and thinly sliced
2 teaspoons honey
1 tablespoon chia seeds (optional)
¼ cup pomegranate seeds (optional)

1. In 2 small glasses or ramekins, create alternating layers of yogurt and granola, about 4 layers, ending with granola.
2. Cut the top and bottom off the grapefruit and oranges and then slice away the remaining peel and white pith. On a steady cutting board, carefully cut the fruit into segments and arrange on top of the parfait.
3. Add the apple and drizzle with the honey.
4. Top with the chia seeds (if using) and pomegranate seeds (if using).

30 MINUTES OR LESS

ONE POT

PREP TIME: 15 MINUTES

SMART SHOPPING:
Any citrus will work in this recipe, so it's fun to branch out and try items like blood oranges, Cara Cara oranges, pomelos—whatever is in season.

PER SERVING:
CALORIES: 564;
FAT: 11G; PROTEIN: 22G;
CARBOHYDRATES: 101G;
FIBER: 11G; SODIUM: 226MG

Crêpes with Mint-and-Pea Pesto

These crêpes are a lovely alternative to the usual weekend brunch fare. Peas and mint are a classic combination, and goat cheese just sends this dish over the top.

30 MINUTES OR LESS

ONE POT

PREP TIME: 15 MINUTES

USE IT UP:

Enjoy any leftover crêpes for breakfast or dessert. Fill them with chocolate-hazelnut butter, strawberries, and honey, and top with whipped cream or yogurt, or fill them with egg salad or tempeh salad for a filling lunch.

PER SERVING:
CALORIES: 717;
FAT: 45G; PROTEIN: 31G;
CARBOHYDRATES: 52G;
FIBER: 12G; SODIUM: 819MG

1 cup loosely packed fresh mint
  leaves, plus more for garnish
3 medium scallions, green and white parts
1½ cups frozen green peas, thawed,
  plus more for garnish
½ cup blanched almonds, toasted
Juice of 1 medium lemon
1 tablespoon olive oil
½ teaspoon kosher salt
¼ teaspoon black pepper
4 to 6 ready-made crêpes
4 ounces goat cheese
Grated zest of 1 medium lemon

1. To make the pesto, in a food processor, combine the mint, scallions, peas, almonds, lemon juice, oil, salt, and pepper. Blend until well incorporated but not totally smooth.
2. Unfold a crêpe and spread about ¼ cup of the pesto onto one side.
3. Add 1 ounce of cheese, fold the crêpe in half, and garnish with mint, a few green peas, and some lemon zest. Repeat until all of the pesto and cheese has been used.

USE IT UP:
GRANOLA

Granola's sweet-and-salty crunch is perfect for breakfast dishes like Banana-Oat Smoothie Bowls (page 23). But why stop there? Granola makes for a fantastic topper for almost any salad with a vinaigrette dressing, like Celery, Apple, and Blue Cheese Chopped Salad with Walnuts (page 38). It can also add texture and crunch to a smooth soup (such as Carrot-Ginger Soup, page 71).

For a daytime snack, mix 1 cup granola with ¼ cup raisins, ¼ cup sliced almonds, ¼ cup dark chocolate chips, and ¼ cup roasted peanuts.

You can also set out a smoothie bowl toppings bar with granola, sliced bananas, chia seeds, toasted coconut, nut butter, macadamia nuts, and berries for a fun kitchen activity.

Ravioli Salad
PAGE 41

chapter 3

SALADS AND HANDHELDS

Celery, Apple, and Blue Cheese Chopped Salad with Walnuts

Don't feel like cooking? Not a problem here. This hearty salad requires only one bowl and a little slicing and dicing with a sharp kitchen knife, and soon you're sitting down to eat. We love that this salad makes two hearty portions—or just save some for lunch the next day and make the whole office jealous.

30 MINUTES OR LESS

ONE POT

PREP TIME: 15 MINUTES

USE IT UP:
Blue cheese adds a tangy kick to many dishes. Use it atop a roasted beet and spinach salad, or enjoy it with pears, walnuts, and multigrain crackers as a snack.

PER SERVING:
CALORIES: 541;
FAT: 39G; PROTEIN: 18G;
CARBOHYDRATES: 35G;
FIBER: 6G; SODIUM: 713MG

1 large apple, cored and diced (about 1½ cups)
Juice of 1 medium lemon
2 medium celery stalks, diced (about 1 cup)
1 medium heart of romaine, sliced (about 2 cups)
2 ounces blue cheese, crumbled
½ cup chopped toasted walnuts
1 shallot, finely diced
2 large eggs, hardboiled
1 tablespoon olive oil
1 tablespoon honey
½ teaspoon kosher salt
¼ teaspoon black pepper

In a large mixing bowl, combine the apple, lemon juice, celery, romaine, cheese, walnuts, shallot, eggs, oil, honey, salt, and pepper. Toss until well mixed.

Tempeh Chicken Salad with Walnuts and Grapes

Why did the tempeh cross the road? Because it was following the chicken's lead. We do the same here as we turn classic chicken salad into a stellar vegetarian dish with one simple tweak. Make this for a Saturday lunch, or let it be your lunchbox staple.

1 (8-ounce) package tempeh, diced
½ cup chopped toasted walnuts
1 cup halved red grapes
1 cup sliced celery (2 medium stalks)
2 scallions, green and white parts, sliced
1 tablespoon spicy brown mustard
¼ cup mayonnaise
2 teaspoons apple cider vinegar
¼ teaspoon dried tarragon
½ teaspoon kosher salt
¼ teaspoon black pepper
2 to 3 cups mixed salad greens

1. In a large mixing bowl, combine the tempeh, walnuts, grapes, celery, scallions, mustard, mayonnaise, vinegar, tarragon, salt, and pepper. Toss until well mixed.
2. Serve a generous scoop of the mixture atop the mixed salad greens.

30 MINUTES OR LESS

ONE POT

PREP TIME: 15 MINUTES

SMART SHOPPING: If toasted walnuts aren't available, you can easily toast raw walnuts in the microwave. Spread the nuts on a plate and microwave for 30 seconds at a time until they're fragrant; this takes about 2 minutes.

PER SERVING:
CALORIES: 689;
FAT: 52G; PROTEIN: 30G;
CARBOHYDRATES: 31G;
FIBER: 4.5G; SODIUM: 611MG

Orange and Avocado Salad

This salad is inspired by tapas meals and glasses of grenache the two of us have enjoyed while sitting at our kitchen table. We captured the sweet, savory, and salty vibe of Mediterranean flavors in this one simple-to-prepare salad.

5-INGREDIENT

30 MINUTES OR LESS

ONE POT

PREP TIME: 15 MINUTES

USE IT UP:

Chop the olives finely, and add kosher salt, black pepper, and a little olive oil to make a tapenade. It's great on slices of baguette for an easy appetizer.

PER SERVING:
CALORIES: 389;
FAT: 31G; PROTEIN: 4G;
CARBOHYDRATES: 32G;
FIBER: 13G; SODIUM: 403MG

2 medium oranges, peeled and sliced
2 medium ripe avocados, pitted, peeled, and sliced
½ cup sliced black olives
1 small shallot, sliced
1 teaspoon sherry vinegar or white-wine vinegar
2 teaspoons olive oil
¼ teaspoon kosher salt
⅛ teaspoon black pepper

1. On a serving platter or 2 plates, arrange the oranges, avocados, olives, and shallot.
2. Drizzle the salad with the vinegar and olive oil. Season with the salt and pepper.

Ravioli Salad

You know a salad is good when the main ingredients are ravioli and cheese. We add texture and flavor to this Italian classic with the addition of pesto, which adds an irresistible garlicky kick.

1 (9-ounce) package mini ravioli, cooked according to package instructions and cooled
1 (6-ounce) jar basil pesto
2 medium tomatoes, cored and sliced
½ cup halved cherry tomatoes
4 ounces fresh mozzarella
½ lemon
Kosher salt
Black pepper
Fresh basil, for garnish

1. Toss the cooked ravioli with the pesto.
2. On a platter, arrange the ravioli, sliced tomatoes, and halved tomatoes.
3. Tear the fresh mozzarella into pieces and place it on top.
4. Squeeze the lemon over the dish, add salt and pepper, and garnish with basil leaves.

5-INGREDIENT

30 MINUTES OR LESS

ONE POT

PREP TIME: 10 MINUTES

COOK TIME: 10 MINUTES

PAIR IT:

For a protein-rich side dish, drain and rinse one 15-ounce can of cannellini beans and flavor them simply with 2 cloves of minced garlic, olive oil, kosher salt, and black pepper.

PER SERVING:
CALORIES: 608;
FAT: 43G; PROTEIN: 22G;
CARBOHYDRATES: 33G;
FIBER: 2.5G; SODIUM: 1,121MG

Chickpea "Falafel" Salad

Everyone loves falafel, but making it fresh at home can be time-consuming. We decided that chickpeas look like tiny falafels, so we should just spice them as such and call it a day when we're looking to whip up a quick lunch. We serve the spiced chickpeas over a wonderful parsley-heavy salad with a spicy tahini dressing for our take on the traditional Middle Eastern falafel sandwich that we've loved since we were teenagers.

30 MINUTES OR LESS

PREP TIME: 10 MINUTES

COOK TIME: 20 MINUTES

PAIR IT:

Warm up some white or whole-wheat pita bread for a nice accompaniment to this salad. If you're not into bread at the moment, add some oven-baked French fries as a side. And if you both love dessert, pick up some baklava to share after your salad.

1 (15-ounce) can chickpeas, drained
1 tablespoon olive oil
½ teaspoon ground cumin
½ teaspoon ground coriander
½ teaspoon kosher salt
Juice of 1 lemon
1 tablespoon tahini or creamy peanut butter
2 teaspoons honey
1 tablespoon sriracha
1 heart of romaine, chopped
1 bunch fresh parsley, finely chopped
1 cup diced cucumbers
1 cup diced seeded Roma tomatoes
1 medium shallot, sliced

1. Preheat the oven to 400°F. Line a sheet pan with parchment paper.
2. On the prepared sheet pan, combine the chickpeas, oil, cumin, coriander, and salt. Shake to coat.
3. Transfer the sheet pan to the oven and bake for 20 minutes. Remove from the oven.
4. Meanwhile, to make the dressing, put the lemon juice, tahini, honey, and sriracha in a small bowl. Whisk until combined.

5. In a large bowl, combine the romaine, parsley, cucumbers, tomatoes, and shallot.
6. Top with the warm chickpeas and dressing and serve.

USE IT UP:
A little bit of tahini goes a long way! Use it in place of peanut butter in sauces and dressings. It's a great dip for raw vegetables and goes well with dishes that feature eggplant. We love the trend of adding a tablespoon or two of tahini to desserts such as brownies, blondies, and chocolate chip cookies for more depth of flavor and an interesting counterpoint to sweetness.

PER SERVING:
CALORIES: 383;
FAT: 15G; PROTEIN: 15G;
CARBOHYDRATES: 54G;
FIBER: 13G; SODIUM: 803MG

Warm Egg Roll Salad

Roll with this easy salad, and you'll get even more of that egg roll flavor you love. Whip up this warm, savory dish up to a day ahead of time, and enjoy our sweet and savory "unwrapped" version of a classic Chinese dish.

30 MINUTES OR LESS

ONE POT

PREP TIME: 15 MINUTES

COOK TIME: 15 MINUTES

SWAP IT:

Trade toasted sliced almonds for the wonton strips, and you'll add a good, nutritious crunch to this salad.

PER SERVING:
CALORIES: 342;
FAT: 16G; PROTEIN: 11G;
CARBOHYDRATES: 48G;
FIBER: 7.5G; SODIUM: 662MG

4 cups shredded cabbage
8 ounces cremini mushrooms, smashed
1 cup shredded carrots (about 2 medium)
1 bunch scallions, green and
 white parts separated
Juice of 1 lime
1 tablespoon toasted sesame oil
1 tablespoon maple syrup
1 tablespoon soy sauce
1 garlic clove, minced
1 (½-inch) knob ginger, peeled and grated
½ teaspoon black pepper
1 cup crunchy wonton strips
Sriracha, for serving

1. Preheat the oven to 400°F. Line a large sheet pan with parchment paper.
2. On the prepared sheet pan, combine the cabbage, mushrooms, carrots, white parts of the scallions, lime juice, oil, maple syrup, soy sauce, garlic, ginger, and pepper. Toss to evenly distribute, and spread in a single layer.
3. Transfer the sheet pan to the oven and bake for 15 minutes, or until the cabbage has softened. Remove from the oven.
4. Top with the wonton strips and sriracha to taste.

Corn Chip Salad

Imagine not having to share your nachos—that's the joyous feeling you get with this salad! Plus, dinner is on the table in less than 10 minutes. We predict that y'all will be making this one on the regular.

3 tablespoons sour cream

½ cup salsa

2 medium scallions, sliced, dark green parts reserved for garnish

2 cups small corn chips

1 (15-ounce) can vegetarian chili

1 cup shredded Cheddar cheese

2 cups finely shredded iceberg lettuce

1 ripe avocado, pitted, peeled, and sliced

1 lime, quartered

⅛ teaspoon kosher salt

1. To make the dressing, put the sour cream, salsa, and white and light green parts of the scallions in a medium bowl. Mix until combined.
2. Divide the chips between 2 bowls.
3. Top each bowl with half of the chili and cheese.
4. Microwave each bowl for 2 minutes.
5. Top each bowl with 1 cup of shredded lettuce, half of the avocado, a squeeze of lime, and half of the salt.

30 MINUTES OR LESS

ONE POT

MINIMAL PREP

PREP TIME: 5 MINUTES

COOK TIME: 5 MINUTES

SMART SHOPPING:

Buy a small (15-ounce) jar of salsa that can be used up quickly. We like the Amy's Kitchen brand of lower-sodium chili for this recipe.

PER SERVING:
CALORIES: 800;
FAT: 49G; PROTEIN: 34G;
CARBOHYDRATES: 61G;
FIBER: 17G; SODIUM: 1,614MG

Ginger-Peanut Cabbage Salad

Crunchy napa cabbage is as close to salad greens as a cabbage can get. If you've never tried it, now is the perfect chance. We pair it with a sweet and savory dressing that has a zing of grated ginger in it. Baked tofu that is preseasoned will save you time and effort. This one comes together fast and is gone in a flash.

30 MINUTES OR LESS

ONE POT

PREP TIME: 15 MINUTES

ADD IT:
Garnish with 1 cup wonton strips for extra crunch.

PER SERVING:
CALORIES: 537;
FAT: 37G; PROTEIN: 29G;
CARBOHYDRATES: 28G;
FIBER: 9.5G; SODIUM: 1,125MG

1 tablespoon maple syrup
1 tablespoon soy sauce
1 tablespoon rice vinegar
2 tablespoons mayonnaise
1½ teaspoons grated ginger
1 teaspoon sriracha
6 cups chopped napa cabbage (about ½ head)
1 medium carrot, shredded
1 bunch scallions, green and white parts, sliced
1 (6-ounce) package baked tofu, diced
½ cup chopped peanuts

1. In a large mixing bowl, whisk together the maple syrup, soy sauce, vinegar, mayonnaise, ginger, and sriracha until well mixed.
2. Add the cabbage, carrot, and scallions. Toss to coat.
3. Add the tofu and peanuts on top.

Warm Acorn Squash Salad

The savory flavor from baked squash makes for the perfect salad for fall and winter. You can eat the skin on an acorn squash, so no need to peel it. This recipe is a terrific reason to jump in and try this versatile vegetable.

1 medium acorn squash

1 tablespoon olive oil

1 teaspoon curry powder

½ teaspoon kosher salt

⅓ cup 2 percent Greek yogurt

1 medium scallion, green and white parts, sliced

Juice of 1 medium lime

1 teaspoon honey

2 cups chopped romaine lettuce

¼ cup chopped toasted cashews

1. Preheat the oven to 350°F. Line a sheet pan with parchment paper.
2. Slice the stem end off the acorn squash, and using a spoon, scrape out the seeds. Slice the squash in half lengthwise and then into ½-inch slices.
3. Arrange the slices in a single layer on the prepared sheet pan.
4. Drizzle with the oil and sprinkle with the curry powder and salt.
5. Transfer the sheet pan to the oven and cook for 30 minutes, or until the squash is lightly browned and cooked through. Remove from the oven.
6. To make the yogurt dressing, put the yogurt, scallion, lime juice, and honey in a small bowl. Using a fork, mix until combined.
7. Put the romaine on a serving platter or 2 plates and arrange the squash on top. Top with the yogurt dressing and cashews.

PREP TIME: 10 MINUTES

COOK TIME: 30 MINUTES

SWAP IT:
Substitute butternut, delicata, or kabocha squash for the acorn squash in this recipe. The sweetness of these winter squashes can't be beat.

PER SERVING:
CALORIES: 301;
FAT: 16G; PROTEIN: 9G;
CARBOHYDRATES: 36G;
FIBER: 5G; SODIUM: 309MG

Big Burrito

When you're craving a big burrito, you can totally feel confident about making it yourself—and in less than half the time it takes to go get one. Keep these grocery staples and some cooked rice on hand for a quick fix anytime you get the craving.

30 MINUTES OR LESS

ONE POT

PREP TIME: 10 MINUTES

COOK TIME: 5 MINUTES

SMART SHOPPING:

Keep a box of instant rice on hand. It's perfect in a pinch when you're making Mexican food, stir-fry, or a curry.

PER SERVING (WITHOUT TOPPINGS):
CALORIES: 841;
FAT: 27G; PROTEIN: 36G;
CARBOHYDRATES: 113G;
FIBER: 17G; SODIUM: 1,980MG

2 (12-inch) flour tortillas
1 cup shredded Cheddar cheese
1 cup cooked rice
1 (15-ounce) can black beans, drained and rinsed
2 scallions, green and white parts, sliced
Juice of 1 lime
Hot sauce
½ teaspoon ground cumin
Sour cream, guacamole, and extra
  hot sauce, for serving

1. Place each tortilla on a piece of wax paper and then on a microwave-safe plate.
2. Divide the cheese, rice, beans, scallions, lime juice, hot sauce, and cumin between the 2 tortillas.
3. While still open-face, microwave each burrito for 1 to 2 minutes.
4. To roll, fold opposite sides with the shortest margins so they touch in the middle. Fold one of the sides with the longer margin over the middle, then roll.
5. Use the wax paper to wrap each burrito to help keep it together.
6. Serve the burritos with sour cream, guacamole, and hot sauce, unwrapping them as you eat.

Loaded Microwave Latkes

Latkes are our favorite potato dish. It's really like all your favorite potato flavors in one—crispy on the outside, creamy on the inside, and just begging to be loaded up with all your favorite toppings. Slightly cooking the potato helps it stay together without eggs or bread crumbs. That's snack innovation!

2 medium russet potatoes
½ teaspoon kosher salt
½ teaspoon black pepper
2 tablespoons olive oil
½ cup shredded Cheddar cheese
¼ cup chopped smoked almonds
¼ cup sliced scallions, green and white parts
½ cup sour cream

1. Poke a few holes in the potatoes and wrap each in damp paper towels.
2. Place the potatoes on a microwave-safe plate and microwave for 6 minutes. Let cool.
3. Once cool enough to handle, grate the potatoes on a box grater. Season with the salt and pepper. Discard any potato skin you're left holding.
4. In a skillet, heat the oil over medium heat.
5. Using a ½-cup measure, press the potatoes into 8 to 10 disks.
6. Add the disks to the skillet and cook for about 3 minutes per side, or until golden brown. Remove from the heat. Drain on paper towels.
7. Top the latkes while still warm with the cheese, almonds, and scallions.
8. Serve the latkes with the sour cream on the side.

5-INGREDIENT

30 MINUTES OR LESS

ONE POT

PREP TIME: 15 MINUTES

COOK TIME: 15 MINUTES

SWAP IT:
Feel free to use Greek yogurt in place of the sour cream. Use vegan yogurt and cheese to make this recipe plant-based.

PER SERVING:
CALORIES: 719;
FAT: 41G; PROTEIN: 19G;
CARBOHYDRATES: 74G;
FIBER: 6.5G; SODIUM: 585MG

Kale and Artichoke Tacos

How do you make one of your favorite dips into a verifiable meal? Make it into a taco, that's how! Quickly whip up a batch of our vegan take on traditional spinach-artichoke dip that we serve family-style. Pick up a tortilla, tuck in a spoonful of warm kale and artichoke mixture, and garnish with salsa. You'll make this one again and again.

ONE POT

PREP TIME: 10 MINUTES

COOK TIME: 25 MINUTES

SWAP IT:

If you have spinach or arugula on hand, use one of those hearty greens in place of the kale.

PER SERVING:
CALORIES: 691;
FAT: 20G; PROTEIN: 31G;
CARBOHYDRATES: 108G;
FIBER: 20G; SODIUM: 2,093MG

1 (14-ounce) can quartered
   artichoke hearts, drained
1 bunch lacinato kale, stemmed, leaves chopped
1 (15-ounce) can white beans or Great
   Northern beans, drained and rinsed
1 (5½-ounce) can full-fat coconut milk
Grated zest and juice of 1 lemon
3 garlic cloves, minced
¼ teaspoon red pepper flakes
½ teaspoon kosher salt
½ cup salsa
8 taco-size corn tortillas, warmed

1. Preheat the oven to 350°F.
2. In a medium casserole dish, combine the artichoke hearts, kale, beans, coconut milk, lemon zest, lemon juice, garlic, red pepper flakes, and salt. Mix it all together.
3. Transfer the dish to the oven and bake for 25 minutes, or until the mixture is bubbling at the edges. Remove from the oven.
4. Serve the filling with the salsa and corn tortillas.

Beet Reuben

Some folks only think they don't like beets because they've only had the canned variety. Get ready for a game changer—we promise this recipe will make a believer out of you. Thinly sliced, coriander-and-black-pepper-spiced beets stand in for beef in this classic sammie. Now drop that beet . . . into some water and boil it.

1 large or 2 medium red beets, peeled
1 tablespoon mustard
1 tablespoon ketchup
1 tablespoon mayonnaise
2 tablespoons chopped pickles
½ teaspoon black pepper
½ teaspoon kosher salt
½ teaspoon ground coriander
4 slices rye bread, toasted
4 slices Swiss cheese
1 cup sauerkraut, drained

1. Put the beets in a medium pot. Add enough water just to cover. Bring to a boil over high heat. Cook for 20 minutes. Remove from the heat. Drain and let cool.
2. Meanwhile, to make the dressing, in a small bowl, mix together the mustard, ketchup, mayonnaise, and pickles.
3. Once the beets are cool enough to handle, thinly slice. Season with the pepper, salt, and coriander.
4. Divide the dressing among the 4 bread slices, then assemble the sandwiches: divide the cheese, beets, and sauerkraut between 2 of the bread slices and top with the remaining 2 bread slices.

PREP TIME: 15 MINUTES

COOK TIME: 20 MINUTES

PAIR IT:
Include your favorite potato salad on the side for a filling lunch or dinner.

PER SERVING:
CALORIES: 491;
FAT: 25G; PROTEIN: 23G;
CARBOHYDRATES: 45G;
FIBER: 8G; SODIUM: 1,580MG

French Dip

A friend of ours loves *jus* so much, he drinks it like a shot after his last bite of French dip. You may just do that, too, with this recipe. Rich, meaty portobello mushrooms are braised in wine and thyme to create a savory *jus* you didn't know was possible without meat. Stuff it, dip it, and crush it.

ONE POT

PREP TIME: 10 MINUTES

COOK TIME: 25 MINUTES

USE IT UP:
Add white wine to onions as they caramelize or to cream sauces as they cook to deepen flavor.

PER SERVING:
CALORIES: 694;
FAT: 24G; PROTEIN: 27G;
CARBOHYDRATES: 68G;
FIBER: 5G; SODIUM: 1,720MG

1 tablespoon olive oil
1 medium onion, sliced
8 ounces portobello mushrooms,
 sliced (about 3 medium)
½ teaspoon black pepper
1 teaspoon dried thyme
1 cup white wine
1 cup water
1 tablespoon soy sauce
1 (12-inch) baguette, split horizontally and toasted
4 slices smoked Gouda cheese

1. Heat a large pot over medium-high heat.
2. Stir in the oil and onion. Cook for 5 minutes, or until browned.
3. Add the mushrooms, stir the mixture, and cook for 3 minutes.
4. Add the pepper, thyme, wine, water, and soy sauce.
5. Reduce the heat to low. Cover the pot and simmer for 15 minutes. Remove from the heat.
6. Reserving the liquid, strain the mushroom mixture.
7. Fill each baguette with the mushroom mixture.
8. Top with the cheese. Serve the broth on the side for dipping.

BBQ Baked Bean Burger

Premade veggie burgers may be convenient, but we've created our own version that is just as simple as it is tasty. With essentially two ingredients, beans and oats, these patties can't be beat on simplicity. We added a barbecue slaw to send this one over the top. Add any fixings you like to make it your own.

1 (15-ounce) can vegetarian baked beans, drained
1 cup quick-cooking oats
½ teaspoon kosher salt
½ teaspoon black pepper
2 cups shredded cabbage mix
¼ cup barbecue sauce
2 tablespoons olive oil
4 hamburger buns, toasted

1. In a large bowl, combine the beans, oats, salt, and pepper.
2. Using your clean hands, smash the beans and oats together until a dough forms. No need to smash every bean—it should be rustic. Let rest for 10 minutes so that the moisture has time to distribute.
3. Meanwhile, to make the slaw, in a large bowl, combine the cabbage mix and barbecue sauce.
4. Form the bean and oat dough into 4 patties.
5. Heat a large skillet over medium heat.
6. Pour in the oil and add the patties. Cook for 4 to 5 minutes per side, or until golden brown. Remove from the heat. Drain on paper towels.
7. Serve the patties on the buns piled high with the slaw.

5-INGREDIENT

30 MINUTES OR LESS

PREP TIME: 15 MINUTES

COOK TIME: 10 MINUTES

USE IT UP:

Shredded cabbage is so versatile. Make a jar of sauerkraut, or cook the cabbage with onions for a quick side dish.

PER SERVING (1 BURGER):
CALORIES: 424;
FAT: 10G; PROTEIN: 13G;
CARBOHYDRATES: 72G;
FIBER: 8.5G; SODIUM: 921MG

Kale and Apple Grilled Cheese

Sure, a plain grilled cheese is good, but what if the idea of a grilled cheese grew up a bit and got a job, and that job was making you very, very happy? Enter the simple-to-make, greens-packed, sweet and sour, savory grilled cheese of your dreams. This is one of those gooey, crazy, messy-in-the-best-way sandwiches that is so fun to eat. We think you'll especially love the whimsical addition of sliced apples in this recipe.

30 MINUTES OR LESS

ONE POT

PREP TIME: 10 MINUTES

COOK TIME: 10 MINUTES

SMART SHOPPING:

You will want a crisp, sweet, and tart apple for this recipe, so be choosy for the best result. Try to seek out Pink Lady apples for this sandwich—they have just the right mix of tart and sweet. Honeycrisp apples also work well here. Reserve very tart apples, like Granny

2 tablespoons olive oil, divided
1 medium shallot, sliced
3 cups stemmed and chopped baby kale
½ teaspoon kosher salt
¼ teaspoon black pepper
1 medium apple, cored and sliced
Juice of ½ medium lemon
1 teaspoon honey
4 slices whole-wheat sandwich bread
4 slices smoked Gouda cheese

1. Heat a skillet over medium heat.
2. Pour in 1 tablespoon of oil and add the shallot, kale, salt, and pepper. Cook for about 5 minutes, or until the kale has wilted. Remove the kale mixture from the skillet and set aside. Remove the skillet from the heat and let cool. Using a paper towel, wipe out the skillet.
3. Assemble the sandwiches: divide the kale mixture, apple, lemon juice, and honey between 2 bread slices.
4. Add 2 slices of cheese to each, then top with the remaining 2 slices of bread.

5. Heat the same skillet over medium heat.
6. Pour in the remaining 1 tablespoon of oil and griddle the sandwiches for 3 to 4 minutes per side, or until golden. Remove from the heat.

Smiths, for pie filling because they won't balance out the savory kale as well as other kinds of apples do.

ADD IT:
Make this grilled cheese your own by adding thinly sliced radishes, pickles, spinach or arugula, or tempeh bacon. The possibilities are endless!

PER SERVING:
CALORIES: 570; FAT: 32G; PROTEIN: 24G; CARBOHYDRATES: 53G; FIBER: 4.5G; SODIUM: 1,073MG

Chickpea Chick'n Sandwich

"What's in a name?" Juliet asks. Plenty, it turns out. A name can give you hints, ideas, even a clue as to what to do. Chickpea . . . chick . . . chicken. It's not a huge philosophical jump. So we made these little chick'n patties from chickpeas, and they are so dang good, you'll be speaking about them in iambic pentameter. This recipe calls for three sandwiches because they're on the small side, so it's likely that you'll want to split the extra one. Now, in our book, that's romance!

30 MINUTES OR LESS

PREP TIME: 10 MINUTES

COOK TIME: 10 MINUTES

ADD IT:

Slice tempeh and baste it with a mixture of miso, soy sauce, olive oil, honey, salt, and pepper. Bake it at 375°F for 15 minutes; it'll add a bacon-y flavor to this sandwich. If you need a shortcut, you can find prepared tempeh bacon in the plant-based refrigerated section of the grocery store.

1 (15-ounce) can chickpeas, drained and rinsed
1 tablespoon apple cider vinegar
½ cup plus 1 tablespoon all-purpose flour
½ teaspoon kosher salt
1 teaspoon black pepper
1 teaspoon smoked paprika
¼ teaspoon garlic powder
½ cup olive oil
3 kaiser rolls, warmed
Mustard, mayonnaise, and sweet or
  dill pickle slices, for garnish

1. In a bowl, using a fork or a potato masher, lightly smash the chickpeas, leaving them mostly whole.
2. Add the vinegar, flour, salt, pepper, paprika, and garlic powder. Mix well.
3. Form the mixture into 3 patties.
4. In a 12-inch skillet, heat the oil over medium heat.

5. Add the patties and cook for 4 to 5 minutes per side, or until golden. Remove from the heat. Drain on paper towels.

6. Serve the patties on the rolls, garnished with mustard, mayonnaise, and pickles.

SWAP IT:
These chick'n patties have myriad uses. Try them tucked into biscuits and drizzled with honey at breakfast for one of our favorite vegetarian-ized Southern treats. Place the patties on top of pasta with marinara sauce at dinner. Add them to Ginger-Peanut Cabbage Salad (page 46) to make it more of a hearty meal instead of a side.

PER SERVING (1 SANDWICH WITHOUT GARNISHES):
CALORIES: 801; FAT: 34G; PROTEIN: 22G; CARBOHYDRATES: 102G; FIBER: 11G; SODIUM: 1,028MG

California Wrap

Jump in the time machine and fly back to last century, when we were just teen-age vegetarians looking for a good meal. This was the dish du jour back then and what Southerners thought people in California would eat at every meal: sprouts, avocado, hummus, and the like. This nostalgic wrap still makes our hearts and tummies happy all these years later.

30 MINUTES OR LESS

ONE POT

PREP TIME: 15 MINUTES

ADD IT:
Plant-based turkey slices or marinated tofu would be welcome and hearty additions to this sandwich.

PER SERVING:
CALORIES: 607;
FAT: 29G; PROTEIN: 17G;
CARBOHYDRATES: 73G;
FIBER: 12G; SODIUM: 1,559MG

2 (12-inch) spinach tortilla wraps
½ cup store-bought hummus
1 cup broccoli sprouts
1 cup sliced cucumbers
2 scallions, green and white parts, sliced
¼ cup Kalamata olives
1 cup halved cherry tomatoes
1 medium ripe avocado, pitted, peeled, and sliced
Juice of 1 lemon
½ teaspoon kosher salt
¼ teaspoon black pepper

1. Put each tortilla on a plate. Divide the hummus, sprouts, cucumbers, scallions, olives, tomatoes, and avocado between the tortillas.
2. Garnish with the lemon juice. Season with the salt and pepper.
3. Fold one side of each tortilla up to keep all the fillings from sliding out and roll it into a wrap.

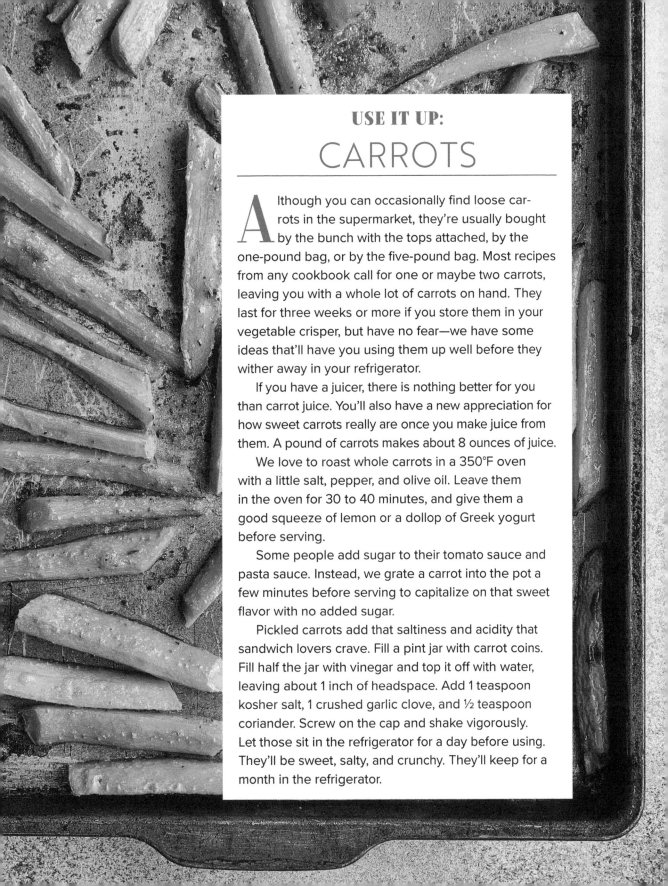

USE IT UP:
CARROTS

Although you can occasionally find loose carrots in the supermarket, they're usually bought by the bunch with the tops attached, by the one-pound bag, or by the five-pound bag. Most recipes from any cookbook call for one or maybe two carrots, leaving you with a whole lot of carrots on hand. They last for three weeks or more if you store them in your vegetable crisper, but have no fear—we have some ideas that'll have you using them up well before they wither away in your refrigerator.

If you have a juicer, there is nothing better for you than carrot juice. You'll also have a new appreciation for how sweet carrots really are once you make juice from them. A pound of carrots makes about 8 ounces of juice.

We love to roast whole carrots in a 350°F oven with a little salt, pepper, and olive oil. Leave them in the oven for 30 to 40 minutes, and give them a good squeeze of lemon or a dollop of Greek yogurt before serving.

Some people add sugar to their tomato sauce and pasta sauce. Instead, we grate a carrot into the pot a few minutes before serving to capitalize on that sweet flavor with no added sugar.

Pickled carrots add that saltiness and acidity that sandwich lovers crave. Fill a pint jar with carrot coins. Fill half the jar with vinegar and top it off with water, leaving about 1 inch of headspace. Add 1 teaspoon kosher salt, 1 crushed garlic clove, and ½ teaspoon coriander. Screw on the cap and shake vigorously. Let those sit in the refrigerator for a day before using. They'll be sweet, salty, and crunchy. They'll keep for a month in the refrigerator.

*Chana
Masala*
PAGE 70

chapter 4

SOUPS AND STEWS

Gnocchi Stew

It's pasta night, but you're tired of the same tired dish. Gnocchi to the rescue! If you're not familiar, gnocchi is an Italian dumpling made mostly from potatoes. Available in many grocery stores, it make this dinnertime soup fast, interesting, and easy.

30 MINUTES OR LESS

PREP TIME: 10 MINUTES

COOK TIME: 20 MINUTES

USE IT UP:
Romano cheese adds depth to any dish. Grate it on top of pastas, soups, beans, or anything that needs a salty, rich kick.

PER SERVING:
CALORIES: 749;
FAT: 13G; PROTEIN: 24G;
CARBOHYDRATES: 123G;
FIBER: 13G; SODIUM: 1,591MG

1 (1-pound) package gnocchi
1 tablespoon olive oil
2 medium celery stalks, sliced
2 medium carrots, sliced
1 large shallot, sliced
4 medium garlic cloves, sliced
½ cup white wine
1 teaspoon Italian seasoning
1 (14½-ounce) can diced fire-roasted tomatoes
Kosher salt
Black pepper
¼ cup grated Romano cheese
1 lemon, cut into wedges

1. Cook the gnocchi according to the package instructions, then drain, reserving 2 cups of pasta cooking water.
2. Meanwhile, heat a medium pot over medium-high heat.
3. Pour in the oil and add the celery, carrots, shallot, and garlic. Cook for 4 to 5 minutes, or until you notice caramelization, a slight browning at the edges.
4. Add the wine and cook until it evaporates.
5. Add the Italian seasoning, tomatoes, reserved pasta cooking water, and gnocchi. Season with salt and pepper. Remove from the heat.
6. Top with the cheese and garnish with a lemon wedge.

White Chili

Salsa has almost all of the flavor you need in any chili recipe, so why not start there and add some meaty components and toppings? We make this unique chili with tomatillo salsa and white beans. Just smash the mushrooms with your hands for an amazing texture. Simple, smart, and scrumptious, it's quite the combo.

1 tablespoon olive oil
1 (8-ounce) package white button
   mushrooms, smashed
1 medium yellow bell pepper, diced
1 (15-ounce) can cannellini beans
1 (16-ounce) jar tomatillo salsa
½ cup sour cream

1. In a medium pot, combine the oil and mush-rooms. Cook over high heat for 5 minutes, or until most of the liquid has cooked off.
2. Add the bell pepper and cook for 5 minutes.
3. Add the beans with their liquid and the salsa and stir.
4. Reduce the heat to a simmer. Cook for 10 minutes. Remove from the heat.
5. Serve the chili warm dolloped with the sour cream.

5-INGREDIENT

30 MINUTES OR LESS

ONE POT

PREP TIME: 10 MINUTES

COOK TIME: 20 MINUTES

ADD IT:
Add a scoop of rice to each bowl to make this dish a complete protein with all of the amino acids.

PER SERVING:
CALORIES: 437;
FAT: 18G; PROTEIN: 16G;
CARBOHYDRATES: 52G;
FIBER: 18G; SODIUM: 1,892MG

Weeknight Ramen

Those packs of ramen noodles need to get a little dressed up for the dinner party, and we've got just the solution. Add a plethora of cooked, raw, and pickled vegetables to make plain old noodles something delicious.

30 MINUTES OR LESS

PREP TIME: 15 MINUTES

COOK TIME: 15 MINUTES

ADD IT:

For extra protein, add a soft-boiled egg or diced firm tofu.

PER SERVING:
CALORIES: 742;
FAT: 30G; PROTEIN: 18G;
CARBOHYDRATES: 110G;
FIBER: 10G; SODIUM: 2,984MG

1 tablespoon toasted sesame oil
1 (3½-ounce) package shiitake
　mushrooms, stemmed
1 tablespoon soy sauce
1 tablespoon maple syrup
3 (3-ounce) packages instant ramen
1 medium red bell pepper, sliced
1 pint grape or cherry tomatoes, halved
2 scallions, green and white parts, sliced
1 medium carrot, shredded
¼ cup kimchi
1 sheet nori, cut in half

1. Heat a medium skillet over high heat.
2. Pour in the oil and add the mushrooms. Cook for 3 minutes per side. Remove from the heat.
3. Add the soy sauce and maple syrup.
4. Make the ramen and broth according to the package instructions. Remove from the heat.
5. Divide the noodles and broth between 2 bowls.
6. Garnish each bowl with the mushrooms, bell pepper, tomatoes, scallions, carrot, kimchi, and nori.

Black Bean Soup

This soup is our go-to lunch or dinner when we're in a hurry. It's two steps: just blend and heat and you're ready to eat. The depth comes from chipotle peppers in a can, which are just smoked jalapeños with garlic and tomato sauce. Yes, they're spicy, but they also add a smoky depth of flavor.

1 (14½-ounce) can diced tomatoes

1 (15-ounce) can black beans

1 vegetarian bouillon cube

2 garlic cloves

1 medium canned chipotle pepper in adobo sauce

1 teaspoon apple cider vinegar

1 teaspoon ground cumin

1 teaspoon ground coriander

2 tablespoons sour cream

Hot sauce, for serving

1. In a blender, combine the tomatoes with their liquid, beans with their liquid, bouillon cube, garlic, chipotle pepper, vinegar, cumin, and coriander. Blend until smooth.
2. Pour the mixture into a medium pot and warm over medium heat. Remove from the heat.
3. Serve the soup warm garnished with the sour cream and hot sauce.

30 MINUTES OR LESS

MINIMAL PREP

PREP TIME: 5 MINUTES

COOK TIME: 5 MINUTES

USE IT UP:

Store the remaining chipotle peppers in an airtight container in the refrigerator for up to 2 months and use them in quesadillas or Smoky Yellow Split Pea Soup (page 76).

PER SERVING:
CALORIES: 282;
FAT: 4G; PROTEIN: 16G;
CARBOHYDRATES: 47G;
FIBER: 16G; SODIUM: 1,800MG

Roasted Butternut Squash Bisque

Maybe you've seen giant butternut squashes in the grocery store but have been unsure of how to cook with them. Basically, it's a lot like baking a potato. You just need to be careful when cutting open such a big vegetable; make sure you have a steady surface and a good knife. We like to cut butternut squash into two large pieces, first dividing the bulbous end from the stem, then cutting it lengthwise and scraping out the seeds; do it this way, and you'll have flat surfaces to work with and a much easier prep. Butternuts are smooth, sweet as honey, and delicious, so the effort is worth it. Get outside your comfort zone and make this restaurant-style bisque.

5-INGREDIENT

PREP TIME: 10 MINUTES

COOK TIME: 40 MINUTES

SWAP IT:
Use dried sage in place of the thyme for a stronger flavor.

1 medium butternut squash, halved or quartered and seeded
1 medium onion, halved
1 teaspoon olive oil
½ teaspoon kosher salt
¼ teaspoon black pepper
½ cup 2 percent Greek yogurt
1 cup water
1 vegetarian bouillon cube
½ teaspoon dried thyme

1. Preheat the oven to 400°F.
2. Place the squash and onion on a sheet pan and drizzle with the oil.
3. Transfer the sheet pan to the oven and roast for 30 minutes. Remove from the oven. Let cool.
4. Once cool enough to handle, scrape out the soft squash flesh and discard the skin. Discard the onion skin.

5. In a blender or food processor, combine the squash, onion, salt, pepper, yogurt, water, bouillon cube, and thyme. Blend until smooth. Transfer to a medium pot.
6. Gently warm the bisque over medium-low heat, being careful not to let it boil. Remove from the heat. Serve warm.

ADD IT:
Garnish with fresh thyme leaves, a swirl of Greek yogurt, and toasted pine nuts for a dressed-up version of this bisque. To add a standout savory flavor, fry some fresh sage for a garnish. In a skillet, heat olive oil over medium heat, and using tongs, carefully drop in the sage leaves one at a time. When they shrink and curl a bit, use the tongs to remove them from the skillet and place them on a paper towel–lined plate to drain and cool before using.

PER SERVING:
CALORIES: 312;
FAT: 4.5G; PROTEIN: 12G;
CARBOHYDRATES: 64G;
FIBER: 10G; SODIUM: 952MG

Mushroom and Potato Stew

This soup is a time machine! It has all the ingredients from the cans of vegetable stew that you remember from your childhood, but you've made it yourself, and it's incredibly flavorful. The secret is to add just enough liquid so that it's not too watery but all of that wonderful vegetable flavor shines through.

ONE POT

PREP TIME: 15 MINUTES

COOK TIME: 25 MINUTES

PAIR IT:

You can't go wrong with a thick slice of rustic bread with this bowl of soup. Feeling cheesy? Make grilled cheese sandwiches to go with the soup.

PER SERVING:
CALORIES: 249;
FAT: 8G; PROTEIN: 7G;
CARBOHYDRATES: 40G;
FIBER: 8G; SODIUM: 733MG

1 tablespoon olive oil
1 small onion, diced
2 medium celery stalks, sliced
2 medium carrots, diced
1 medium red bell pepper, diced
2 medium portobello mushrooms, diced
1 medium russet potato, peeled and diced
1 vegetarian bouillon cube
1 heaping tablespoon tomato paste
4 dashes vinegar-based hot sauce
1½ to 2 cups water

1. Heat a medium pot over medium-high heat.
2. Pour in the oil and add the onion, celery, carrots, bell pepper, mushrooms, and potato. Cook for 5 minutes, or until the vegetables start to brown.
3. Add the bouillon cube, tomato paste, hot sauce, and enough water to just cover the vegetables. Stir. Bring to a boil.
4. Reduce the heat to a simmer. Cover the pot and cook for 10 to 15 minutes, or until the potato is tender. Remove from the heat.

Pesto Tomato Soup

The sweetness from the carrots, the herbaceous notes from the pesto, the savory notes from the tomatoes and cheese, the heat of the red pepper flakes—this is not your run-of-the-mill tomato soup! The grated carrots add a sweet note and some extra nutrients.

1 tablespoon olive oil
4 medium garlic cloves, sliced
1 (28-ounce) can crushed tomatoes
2 medium carrots, grated
1 cup water
1 (3½-ounce) jar pesto
⅛ teaspoon red pepper flakes
⅛ cup shredded Romano cheese,
  plus more for serving

1. In a medium pot, combine the oil and garlic. Cook over medium-high heat, keeping a close eye on it so that the garlic doesn't burn.
2. As the garlic starts to brown, add the tomatoes, carrots, water, pesto, red pepper flakes, and cheese. Cover the pot and cook for 10 to 15 minutes, or until the carrots soften. Remove from the heat.
3. Serve the soup warm with more cheese on the side.

30 MINUTES OR LESS

ONE POT

PREP TIME: 10 MINUTES

COOK TIME: 15 MINUTES

PAIR IT:
We love chickpeas or cooked brown rice scooped onto this amazing soup to take it from a simple lunch to a more hearty dinner.

PER SERVING:
CALORIES: 476;
FAT: 27G; PROTEIN: 15G;
CARBOHYDRATES: 43G;
FIBER: 13G; SODIUM: 1,297MG

Chana Masala

Whether you're new to Indian food or you're a loyal weekly visitor to your local Indian restaurant, you will love making this dish! It satisfies that craving for the lovely warm spices that you get from chana masala. It looks like a lot of ingredients here, but it's mostly spices. That's what gives this dish such a complex and interesting flavor.

30 MINUTES OR LESS

MINIMAL PREP

PREP TIME: 5 MINUTES

COOK TIME: 20 MINUTES

PAIR IT:

Naan, a traditional Indian flatbread, is available at most grocery stores these days. It's the perfect partner for this dish.

PER SERVING:
CALORIES: 531;
FAT: 12G; PROTEIN: 18G;
CARBOHYDRATES: 90G;
FIBER: 14G; SODIUM: 1,482MG

1 (14½-ounce) can diced tomatoes
1 medium onion
1 (1-inch) knob ginger, peeled
1 tablespoon sriracha
1 tablespoon olive oil
½ teaspoon kosher salt
½ teaspoon black pepper
½ teaspoon ground cinnamon
½ teaspoon ground cumin
½ teaspoon ground coriander
½ teaspoon ground turmeric or curry powder
1 (15-ounce) can chickpeas
1½ cups cooked basmati rice

1. In a blender or food processor, combine the tomatoes, onion, ginger, and sriracha. Blend until smooth.
2. In a medium pan, combine the oil, salt, pepper, cinnamon, cumin, coriander, and turmeric. Heat over medium heat until you smell the spices toasting.
3. Add the tomato mixture and cook for 5 minutes, or until a thick paste forms.
4. Add the chickpeas with their liquid. Cover the pan and simmer for 10 minutes. Remove from the heat.
5. Serve the chana masala warm over the rice.

Carrot-Ginger Soup

Shortcuts that don't sacrifice flavor are our favorite kitchen hacks. Here, we microwave the carrots to get them soft enough to blend. You'll be amazed by what the cashews add to this dish, and we've found that there's really no need to soak them ahead of time.

3 cups coarsely chopped carrots
½ cup raw cashews
1 (1-inch) knob ginger, peeled and minced
½ cup water, plus about 1½ cups for thinning
Grated zest and juice of 1 lime
1 vegetarian bouillon cube
2 teaspoons honey
½ cup Greek yogurt

1. Put the carrots in a microwave-safe dish. Cover and microwave for 6 minutes. Let stand, covered, for another 10 minutes to allow the carrots to cook through and cool a bit.
2. In a blender, combine the carrots, cashews, ginger, ½ cup of water, the lime zest, lime juice, bouillon cube, and honey. Blend until smooth.
3. Add enough water to get to a consistency similar to pancake batter.
4. Serve the soup with a dollop of yogurt.

30 MINUTES OR LESS

MINIMAL PREP

PREP TIME: 5 MINUTES

COOK TIME: 15 MINUTES

SMART SHOPPING:

We love using local honey in our recipes and often purchase a large jar. Over time, we decant it into a smaller honey bear container for ease of use—and also to save money.

PER SERVING:
CALORIES: 338;
FAT: 16G; PROTEIN: 13G;
CARBOHYDRATES: 37G;
FIBER: 6.5G; SODIUM: 790MG

Confetti Corn Chowder

This recipe combines two of our favorite comfort foods—carbs and soup! With the combination of corn and potato, this soup doubles the carbohydrates for satisfying nourishment. We like how the red pepper and chives add some contrasting color to the mix so that this chowder looks as good as it tastes. This recipe makes the perfect amount for two, but it's easy to scale it up when you have guests.

PREP TIME: 10 MINUTES

COOK TIME: 25 MINUTES

SWAP IT:

If you don't have chipotles on hand, just sub in 1 chopped seeded jalapeño pepper.

ADD IT:

Enjoy cheese quesadillas along with your chowder for a hearty lunch or dinner.

PER SERVING (WITHOUT GARNISHES):
CALORIES: 328;
FAT: 10G; PROTEIN: 8G;
CARBOHYDRATES: 47G;
FIBER: 5G; SODIUM: 211MG

1 tablespoon olive oil
1 small white onion, diced
½ teaspoon ground cumin
3 garlic cloves, chopped
1 canned chipotle pepper in adobo sauce
½ cup white wine
½ cup water
½ cup whole milk
1 teaspoon distilled white vinegar
1½ cups frozen organic corn kernels, divided
1 Yukon Gold potato, diced
1 red bell pepper, diced
Kosher salt
Black pepper
Chopped fresh chives, for garnish
Sour cream, for serving

1. In a medium pot, heat the oil over medium-high heat until it shimmers.
2. Add the onion and cook for about 7 minutes, or until translucent and soft.
3. Add the cumin and garlic. Cook for about 1 minute, or until fragrant.
4. Add the chipotle pepper and wine. Cook until the wine has reduced by more than half.

5. In a blender, combine the water, milk, vinegar, and 1 cup of frozen corn. Blend the mixture.
6. Add the mixture to the pot along with the potato and bell pepper.
7. Put the remaining ½ cup of corn in a medium pan. Cook over high heat, stirring occasionally, for 4 minutes, or until nicely browned. Remove from the heat.
8. Add the corn to the pot.
9. Reduce the heat to low. Cover the pot and cook for 15 minutes, or until the potato is tender. Remove from the heat. Season with salt and pepper.
10. Garnish with chives and sour cream.

Baked Potato Soup

The trick here is the roasted garlic. It gives this soup a deep, savory flavor that you'll crave. We leave the potato skin on the potatoes and include plenty of chunks.

MINIMAL PREP

PREP TIME: 5 MINUTES

COOK TIME: 50 MINUTES

USE IT UP:
In our house, sour cream and Greek yogurt are pretty interchangeable. Use up your sour cream before you stock up on more yogurt.

PER SERVING:
CALORIES: 407;
FAT: 16G; PROTEIN: 15G;
CARBOHYDRATES: 55G;
FIBER: 3.5G; SODIUM: 761MG

1 large head garlic
2 medium russet potatoes
1 tablespoon unsalted butter
1 vegetarian bouillon cube
½ teaspoon black pepper
2 cups 2 percent milk
4 dashes hot sauce
¼ cup sour cream
2 scallions, green and white parts, sliced

1. Preheat the oven to 350°F.
2. Cut the top third off the garlic, discard the top, and wrap the rest in aluminum foil.
3. Using a sharp knife, poke a few holes in the potatoes. Put the potatoes and garlic on a sheet pan.
4. Transfer the sheet pan to the oven and bake for 40 minutes, or until a butter knife easily pierces the center of a potato. Remove from the oven. Let cool.
5. Once the garlic is cool enough to handle, squeeze the flesh out of the bulb into a medium pot.
6. Add the butter and potatoes. Using a potato masher or large fork, mash the potatoes and garlic. Leave some chunks.
7. Add the bouillon cube, pepper, milk, and hot sauce.
8. Warm the soup over medium heat, stirring to assure it doesn't come to a boil. Remove from the heat. Serve warm with sour cream and scallions.

Chilled Honeydew Soup with Peanut Pesto

You've never had anything like this particular chilled soup. We promise. It borrows some Thai flavor combinations with the citrus, lemongrass, cilantro, and peanuts but is presented in a new way. The tofu adds some protein and gives a creamy base for the melon flavors.

1 medium honeydew, peeled, seeded, and diced
Juice of 1 medium lemon
1 (12.3-ounce) package firm tofu
1 stalk lemongrass
1 tablespoon maple syrup
1 teaspoon kosher salt
1 cup fresh cilantro
½ cup peanuts
2 scallions, green and white parts, chopped
1 teaspoon soy sauce
1 teaspoon sriracha, plus more for garnish

1. In a food processor, combine the honeydew, lemon juice, tofu, lemongrass, maple syrup, and salt. Blend until smooth.
2. Place the mixture into a mesh strainer or food mill to strain out the fibers of lemongrass and stubborn bits of melon. Set aside in the refrigerator to chill.
3. Quickly rinse the food processor bowl. To create the pesto, add the cilantro, peanuts, scallions, soy sauce, and sriracha. Pulse until finely chopped.
4. Serve the soup with a few tablespoons of the pesto and a swirl of sriracha.

30 MINUTES OR LESS

ONE POT

PREP TIME: 20 MINUTES

SMART SHOPPING:
Look for a honeydew melon that's fragrant at the stem end. The more fragrant, the more flavor!

PER SERVING:
CALORIES: 697;
FAT: 24G; PROTEIN: 27G;
CARBOHYDRATES: 106G;
FIBER: 11G; SODIUM: 1,149MG

Smoky Yellow Split Pea Soup

Ham isn't an option at our house, so we use a combination of mushrooms and chipotle peppers to give that meaty texture and smoky flavor to this soup. All this deliciousness is enveloped in comforting yellow split peas that are falling-apart tender.

ONE POT

PREP TIME: 20 MINUTES

COOK TIME: 55 MINUTES

SWAP IT:

Green split peas and red lentils also work well in this recipe.

PER SERVING:
CALORIES: 488;
FAT: 9.5G; PROTEIN: 26G;
CARBOHYDRATES: 77G;
FIBER: 27G; SODIUM: 995MG

1 tablespoon olive oil
1 celery stalk, diced
1 small onion, diced
1 medium carrot, diced
1 (8-ounce) package white mushrooms, diced
1 cup dry yellow split peas
1 vegetarian bouillon cube
1 canned chipotle pepper in adobo sauce, minced
1 tablespoon apple cider vinegar
2 bay leaves
2½ cups water
½ teaspoon kosher salt
¼ cup chopped curly parsley

1. Heat a medium pot over high heat.
2. Pour in the oil and add the celery, onion, and carrot. Cook for 5 minutes, or until the onion starts to brown.
3. Add the mushrooms, split peas, bouillon cube, chipotle pepper, vinegar, bay leaves, water, and salt. Bring to a boil.
4. Reduce the heat to a simmer. Cover the pot and cook, stirring every so often to avoid scorching, for 45 minutes, or until the peas are soft all the way through. Remove from the heat.
5. Serve the soup warm garnished with the parsley.

Three Pepper and Sweet Potato Stew

Borrowing from the bold flavors of Ethiopia and Nigeria, this vegetable-packed stew is light and bright. It's simply perfect to enjoy on that first cool day of fall or as a go-to winter dinner. The fresh rosemary really adds the perfect herbal note to this dish, and the grated ginger combined with the jalapeño brings just enough heat.

1 tablespoon olive oil
4 medium garlic cloves, minced
1 (½-inch) knob ginger, peeled and grated
1 tablespoon fresh chopped rosemary leaves
1 vegetarian bouillon cube
1 (15-ounce) can crushed fire-roasted tomatoes
1½ cups water
Grated zest and juice of 1 medium lemon
2 medium red bell peppers, diced
1 medium jalapeño, minced
1 small sweet potato, peeled and diced
1 tablespoon honey
¼ cup chopped peanuts

1. In a medium pot, combine the oil, garlic, and ginger. Cook over medium-high heat for a few minutes, or until the garlic and ginger become fragrant.
2. Add the rosemary, bouillon cube, tomatoes, water, lemon zest, lemon juice, bell peppers, jalapeño, sweet potato, and honey. Bring to a boil.
3. Reduce the heat to a simmer. Cover the pot and cook for 15 minutes, or until the sweet potato is tender. Remove from the heat.
4. Top with the peanuts and serve warm.

30 MINUTES OR LESS

ONE POT

PREP TIME: 10 MINUTES

COOK TIME: 20 MINUTES

SMART SHOPPING:
We always have cans of crushed and diced tomatoes in the cupboard. Be sure to have some cans of fire-roasted tomatoes on hand to add a distinctive smoky kick to your dishes.

PER SERVING:
CALORIES: 387;
FAT: 17G; PROTEIN: 11G;
CARBOHYDRATES: 51G;
FIBER: 11G; SODIUM: 1,122MG

Ravioli Vegetable Soup

We put this dish together at the end of a long day while we talked about all that had transpired. When we tasted our creation, we both agreed it *had to* be in the book. It's that good! Choose your favorite ravioli to go in this soup. We love cheese- or mushroom-stuffed ravioli, but feel free to experiment with ones filled with butternut squash or spinach.

30 MINUTES OR LESS

PREP TIME: 15 MINUTES

COOK TIME: 15 MINUTES

ADD IT:

A hearty grating of Romano cheese, which is reliably vegetarian, is a lovely addition on top of this soup; a can of chickpeas added to the mix would be excellent, as well. And some warm, crusty bread with butter really makes a soup night feel like a more satisfying dinner at a restaurant.

1 tablespoon olive oil
1 small red bell pepper, diced
1 medium carrot, diced
1 medium shallot, diced
4 garlic cloves, sliced
½ cup rosé or white wine
1 (14½-ounce) can diced fire-roasted tomatoes
1½ cups water
1 vegetarian bouillon cube
¼ cup chopped fresh parsley, plus more for garnish
1 (9-ounce) package cheese or mushroom ravioli

1. In a medium pot, combine the oil, bell pepper, carrot, shallot, and garlic. Cook over high heat, stirring often, for 5 minutes, or until the shallot starts to brown.
2. Add the wine and cook for about 3 minutes, or until mostly evaporated.
3. Add the tomatoes with their liquid, the water, bouillon cube, and ¼ cup of parsley. Bring to a boil.
4. Reduce the heat to a simmer and cover the pot.
5. In a separate pot, cook the ravioli according to the package instructions.

6. Add the ravioli to the soup just before serving. Remove from the heat.
7. Serve the soup warm garnished with a sprinkle of parsley.

SMART SHOPPING: It takes a little extra effort to find, but more and more often, vegan or gluten-free ravioli can be procured at grocery stores these days. Use the ravioli your partner prefers or requires and see how you like it, or make a couple of different kinds of ravioli for this recipe.

PER SERVING:
CALORIES: 505;
FAT: 13G; PROTEIN: 20G;
CARBOHYDRATES: 67G;
FIBER: 4G; SODIUM: 1,128MG

Curried Cauliflower Soup

It is a tradition in our family to enjoy cauliflower soup around the holidays. It's become the norm to have one pot made with chicken stock and one with vegetarian stock so that everyone may partake. The curry powder and coconut milk we use here in our version offer an inspired new take on classic cauli soup.

30 MINUTES OR LESS

ONE POT

MINIMAL PREP

PREP TIME: 5 MINUTES

COOK TIME: 25 MINUTES

SMART SHOPPING:

Look for a head of cauliflower that's on the smaller side when you are cooking for two so that there's nothing left over. You may use white, yellow, purple, or green cauliflower for this recipe—your choice!

PER SERVING:
CALORIES: 298;
FAT: 19G; PROTEIN: 7G;
CARBOHYDRATES: 32G;
FIBER: 8G; SODIUM: 785MG

1 tablespoon olive oil
1 medium onion, diced
1 small head cauliflower, chopped
1 tablespoon curry powder
1 (13½-ounce) can light coconut milk
Juice of ½ lemon
1 vegetarian bouillon cube
1½ cups water

1. Heat a medium pot over high heat.
2. Pour in the oil and add the onion. Cook, stirring often, for 5 minutes, or until the onion starts to brown.
3. Add the cauliflower, curry powder, coconut milk, lemon juice, bouillon cube, and water. Bring to a boil.
4. Reduce the heat to a simmer. Cover the pot and cook for 15 minutes, or until the cauliflower is tender. Remove from the heat. Serve warm.

USE IT UP:

GREEK YOGURT

Greek yogurt contains protein, probiotics, and an array of nutrients, meaning it's an excellent ingredient to add to your rotation a few days a week. It's also a chameleon in the kitchen.

Sure, it's terrific in Yogurt, Citrus, and Granola Parfait (page 33). But do you know you can crumble some blue cheese into Greek yogurt to make a tangy-but-healthy dressing? Try Greek yogurt on your breakfast tacos, or any tacos for that matter, in place of sour cream. Or add a spoonful to boxed mac and cheese to give it some acidity and richness.

Our favorite thing to do with a leftover cup of Greek yogurt is stir in 1 teaspoon chopped dill, 1 tablespoon chopped parsley, 1 sliced scallion, a squeeze of lemon, 1 teaspoon honey, and salt and black pepper to taste to make Greek yogurt ranch dip. Get out some crudités and go to town.

In addition, we often use Greek yogurt to top desserts. Just take ½ cup Greek yogurt and whisk in 1 tablespoon maple syrup, ½ teaspoon vanilla extract or the inside of a vanilla bean, a squeeze of lemon, and a pinch of sea salt for a sweet and tangy topping for fruit cobblers and pies.

Grandma Pie
PAGE 86

HEARTY MAINS

Fancy Overstuffed Quesadillas

We say anything is better when it's smothered in cheese and folded into a crispy tortilla. The more filling you can stuff inside, the better. These big boys stretch the limits of your average tortilla and are filled with all of the good stuff: fresh asparagus, good-for-you spinach, and sweet red bell pepper.

30 MINUTES OR LESS

ONE POT

MINIMAL PREP

PREP TIME: 5 MINUTES

COOK TIME: 15 MINUTES

ADD IT:
Add some avocado slices to put these quesadillas over the top.

PER SERVING:
CALORIES: 594;
FAT: 24G; PROTEIN: 26G;
CARBOHYDRATES: 70G;
FIBER: 9.5G; SODIUM: 1,382MG

1 tablespoon olive oil
1 medium red bell pepper, sliced
1 bunch asparagus, trimmed and
   cut into 1-inch pieces
½ teaspoon kosher salt
¼ teaspoon red pepper flakes
3 garlic cloves, sliced
1 (5-ounce) package fresh spinach
2 cups shredded smoked provolone cheese
2 (12-inch) flour tortillas
¼ cup Greek yogurt
Mexican hot sauce, for serving

1. Heat a large skillet over high heat.
2. Pour in the oil and add the bell pepper, aspara-gus, salt, and red pepper flakes. Cook, stirring every few seconds, for 3 minutes, or until the vegetables start to brown.
3. Add the garlic and cook for 1 minute.
4. Add the spinach and cook for 1 minute, or until the spinach has wilted. Remove from the heat. Remove the vegetables from the skillet and set aside.
5. Let the skillet cool, then carefully wipe with a paper towel.

6. Divide the vegetables and cheese between the 2 tortillas and fold each in half.
7. Reheat the skillet over medium heat. Add the quesadillas and cook for 4 minutes per side, or until golden. Remove from the heat.
8. Serve the quesadillas warm with the yogurt on the side and a dash of hot sauce.

Grandma Pie

We built a pizza oven at our house. It's true! That's how much we love pizza. Sometimes, on a nice night when we have the time, we go through all the painstaking steps to make a sauce from scratch, use a sourdough starter, and build a wood fire. Other nights we make this amazingly simple, humble, little, classic square pizza that frankly is just as delicious.

5-INGREDIENT

PREP TIME: 50 MINUTES

COOK TIME: 20 MINUTES

SMART SHOPPING:
By using rapid-rise yeast rather than active dry yeast for this recipe, you're saving time. Who wants to sit around forever waiting for dough to rise?

1 tablespoon olive oil
1½ cups all-purpose flour
1 (¼-ounce) package rapid-rise yeast
6 ounces warm water
1 teaspoon kosher salt
1 (14-ounce) jar pizza sauce, divided
1½ cups shredded whole-milk mozzarella cheese

1. Preheat the oven to 500°F. Line a rimmed sheet pan with parchment paper. Brush with the oil.
2. To make the dough, in a bowl, combine the flour, yeast, water, and salt until all the water is just incorporated. Cover the dough with a kitchen towel and let rise for 30 minutes.
3. Using damp hands, press the dough into the prepared sheet pan. Cover loosely with aluminum foil. Let rise for another 15 minutes.
4. Uncover and spread about 1 cup of pizza sauce on top of the dough. Reserve the remaining sauce.

5. Add the cheese. Transfer the sheet pan to the oven and cook for 15 to 20 minutes, or until the edges are puffed and toasty and the cheese is melted and bubbly. Remove from the oven. Let cool for 10 minutes.

6. Cut the pizza into squares. Serve warm with the reserved sauce for dipping your crust.

ADD IT:

We love a half-this-and-half-that pizza night so we each get to claim a side and choose the toppings we like best. Set out a selection of toppings, such as sliced black olives, roasted garlic, plant-based pepperoni or sausage, buffalo mozzarella, sliced mushrooms, pineapple, and sliced onion, and have fun creating two versions of the best pizza ever.

PER SERVING:
CALORIES: 813;
FAT: 34G; PROTEIN: 32G;
CARBOHYDRATES: 93G;
FIBER:5.5G;SODIUM:1,825MG

Sushi Bowls

Feeling inspired (and a little tired) one weekend night, we thought to ourselves, what if we took all of our favorite vegetarian sushi roll ingredients and layered them in bowls? Use this recipe as is, or swap out ingredients to fit your mood or the season.

PREP TIME: 20 MINUTES

COOK TIME: 25 MINUTES

SWAP IT:

What vegetables do you have in your refrigerator right now? Think about using asparagus, broccoli, or even kohlrabi in place of any of the vegetables in the recipe. The rice base and dressing will make any vegetable sing.

PER SERVING:
CALORIES: 741;
FAT: 34G; PROTEIN: 31G;
CARBOHYDRATES: 81G;
FIBER: 12G; SODIUM: 1,223MG

1 (14-ounce) package extra-firm tofu, cut into 4 slices
1 large portobello mushroom, sliced
2 tablespoons soy sauce, divided
½ teaspoon black pepper
1 tablespoon rice vinegar
1 tablespoon sriracha
1 tablespoon maple syrup
1 tablespoon toasted sesame oil or olive oil
2 cups cooked sushi rice
1 medium carrot, shredded
2 scallions, green and white parts, sliced
1 ripe avocado, pitted, peeled, and sliced
2 sheets toasted nori
2 tablespoons cream cheese

1. Preheat the oven to 400°F. Line a sheet pan with parchment paper.
2. Arrange the tofu and mushroom in a single layer on the prepared sheet pan.
3. Add 1 tablespoon of soy sauce and the pepper on top.
4. Transfer the sheet pan to the oven and bake for 25 minutes, or until the edges of the tofu are crispy. Remove from the oven.

5. To make the dressing, in a medium bowl, whisk together the vinegar, sriracha, remaining 1 tablespoon of soy sauce, the maple syrup, and oil.
6. Divide the rice, tofu, mushroom, carrot, scallions, avocado, nori, and cream cheese between 2 bowls. Serve warm with the dressing on the side.

Veggie Fajitas

First you hear the sizzle, then you see the smoke. You know the feeling—every time someone orders fajitas at a restaurant, you wish that hot plate was headed right to your table. These homemade fajitas with mushrooms, scallions, and peppers will be a game changer for your weeknight meal rotation.

ONE POT

PREP TIME: 20 MINUTES

COOK TIME: 20 MINUTES

USE IT UP:
Make breakfast tacos by topping leftovers with a few scrambled eggs.

1 tablespoon olive oil

1 (8-ounce) package cremini mushrooms, smashed

1 bunch scallions, green and white parts, cut into 1-inch pieces

1 medium red bell pepper, sliced

1 serrano or jalapeño pepper, sliced

2 Roma tomatoes, halved lengthwise

1 tablespoon apple cider vinegar

1 teaspoon ground cumin

½ teaspoon ground coriander

1 teaspoon smoked paprika

1 (16-ounce) jar salsa, divided

1 (15-ounce) can vegetarian refried beans

½ cup shredded smoked Cheddar cheese

6 taco-size tortillas, wrapped together in aluminum foil

Sour cream, guacamole, and hot sauce, for garnish

1. Preheat the oven to 350°F.
2. Heat a medium oven-safe skillet over high heat.
3. Pour in the oil and add the mushrooms, scallions, bell pepper, serrano pepper, and tomatoes. Cook, turning every 30 seconds, for 3 minutes, or until slightly charred.

4. Add the vinegar, cumin, coriander, paprika, and 1 cup of salsa. Stir to mix and warm through. Remove from the heat. Push the mixture to one side of the skillet.
5. Spoon the beans onto the other side of the skillet.
6. Top with the cheese.
7. Transfer the skillet and tortillas to the oven and bake for 10 to 15 minutes, or until the cheese has melted and the beans are heated through. Remove from the oven.
8. Serve the fajitas family-style with the remaining salsa and garnish with sour cream, guacamole, and hot sauce.

ADD IT:
Guacamole is always a good addition! We usually peel and dice 3 firm, just-ripe avocados; add a teaspoon of diced shallot and dashes of salt, black pepper, and red pepper flakes; and squeeze the juice from half an orange over it. Serve the guacamole on the side.

PER SERVING (WITHOUT GARNISHES):
CALORIES: 615;
FAT: 18G; PROTEIN: 28G;
CARBOHYDRATES: 85G;
FIBER: 21G; SODIUM: 2,533MG

Tempeh Bolognese

What are the characteristics of a good Bolognese? It has to be unbelievably savory with a true meaty texture. We get that texture by using tempeh in an unusual way: We crumble the tempeh, and it looks a lot like ground beef in the finished dish. Tempeh really is one of the best plant-based sources of protein around. Feel free to double this recipe and freeze half for another night.

30 MINUTES OR LESS

PREP TIME: 15 MINUTES

COOK TIME: 15 MINUTES

SMART SHOPPING:

Tempeh is available at most grocery stores these days. Look for original soy tempeh, which looks like a pale, textured cake; it's made with only soybeans rather than a mix of beans and grains.

PER SERVING:
CALORIES: 1,152;
FAT: 33G; PROTEIN: 59G;
CARBOHYDRATES: 154G;
FIBER: 20G; SODIUM: 2,112MG

1 tablespoon olive oil
1 medium onion, diced
4 garlic cloves, smashed
½ cup red wine
1 bunch curly kale, stemmed and chopped
1 (8-ounce) package tempeh, crumbled
1 (25-ounce) jar marinara or tomato sauce
¼ teaspoon red pepper flakes
8 ounces spaghetti, cooked according
  to the package instructions
¼ cup grated Romano cheese

1. Heat a medium skillet over medium heat.
2. Pour in the oil and add the onion and garlic. Cook for 5 minutes, or until the onion becomes translucent.
3. Add the wine and kale. Cook for 3 minutes, or until the kale has wilted.
4. Add the tempeh, marinara, and red pepper flakes. Stir to heat through.
5. Add the spaghetti and toss to coat. Remove from the heat.
6. Serve the pasta warm garnished with the cheese.

Skillet Mexican Lasagna

This is the definition of comfort food in our house. It's a mash-up of Italian-style lasagna with Mexican-inspired ingredients and flavors. We use walnuts in place of ground beef here, and it's a simple swap that we think you'll love.

2 garlic cloves

1 cup walnuts

½ teaspoon ground cumin

½ teaspoon ground coriander

½ teaspoon kosher salt

1 tablespoon water

1 cup salsa, divided

4 (10-inch) flour tortillas, divided

1 (15-ounce) can vegetarian refried beans, divided

1 cup shredded Cheddar cheese, divided

1. Preheat the oven to 350°F.
2. In a food processor, combine the garlic, walnuts, cumin, coriander, salt, and water. Pulse the mixture until it looks like ground meat.
3. In a small oven-safe skillet, combine ½ cup of salsa, a tortilla, one-third of the beans, one-third of the walnut mixture, and ¼ cup of cheese.
4. For the second layer, add another tortilla, one-third of the beans, one-third of the walnut mixture, and ¼ cup of cheese.
5. For the third layer, repeat step 4.
6. For the top layer, add the remaining tortilla, remaining ½ cup of salsa, and remaining ¼ cup of cheese.
7. Transfer the skillet to the oven and bake for 20 to 25 minutes, or until the cheese is melted and bubbling. Remove from the oven. Serve warm.

30 MINUTES OR LESS
MINIMAL PREP

PREP TIME: 5 MINUTES

COOK TIME: 25 MINUTES

ADD IT:
You can bling this out to your heart's content. Add sliced radishes, Greek yogurt or sour cream, hot sauce, guacamole, or anything else that catches your fancy.

PER SERVING:
CALORIES: 1,214;
FAT: 61G; PROTEIN: 46G;
CARBOHYDRATES: 124G;
FIBER: 18G; SODIUM: 3,675MG

Creamy Cauliflower Noodles

The old switcheroo! We take that heavy cream–based pasta sauce we all know and love and lighten it up a bit while still keeping the creamy texture that makes it worth eating. This is the antidote for your boring pasta routine. You'll hardly even believe you're eating cauliflower—and the kicker is, the option of adding seasonal vegetables that are steamed or roasted will make this recipe a year-round favorite.

MINIMAL PREP

PREP TIME: 5 MINUTES

COOK TIME: 30 MINUTES

PAIR IT:

Make a side salad by adding a pinch of salt and pepper, a squeeze of lemon, a splash of olive oil, a few grape tomatoes, and a scattering of sliced scallions to your favorite salad greens.

1 (12-ounce) bag cauliflower florets
1 teaspoon Italian seasoning
Grated zest and juice of 1 lemon
1 teaspoon kosher salt
1 cup grated Romano cheese, plus more for garnish
¼ cup raw cashews
6 garlic cloves
3 cups water
¼ teaspoon red pepper flakes
8 ounces pasta of your choice

1. In a medium pot, combine the cauliflower, Italian seasoning, lemon zest, lemon juice, salt, 1 cup of cheese, cashews, garlic, water, and red pepper flakes. Bring to a boil over high heat.
2. Reduce the heat to a simmer. Cover the pot and cook for 20 minutes, or until the cauliflower is very soft. Remove from the heat.
3. Meanwhile, in another pot, cook the pasta according to the package directions.

4. Using an immersion blender, blend the cauliflower mixture smooth. If you do not have an immersion blender, allow the liquid to cool for at least 30 minutes and blend it in small batches in a blender or food processor. Before you blend, take out the insert from the blender lid and cover the opening with a kitchen towel.

5. Toss the sauce with the pasta.

6. Garnish with cheese and serve warm.

ADD IT:

Although this cauliflower pasta dish is quite good on its own, sometimes you may have vegetables on hand to use up, or maybe a more colorful plate appeals to your dinner partner. Add steamed asparagus, green peas, and rainbow carrots to the mix for a springtime take, or top this pasta with roasted butternut squash, sweet onions, and tomatoes for a hearty meal.

PER SERVING:
CALORIES: 782; FAT: 24G; PROTEIN: 38G; CARBOHYDRATES: 103G; FIBER:8.5G;SODIUM:1,428MG

Ranch Sheet Pan Nachos

Sweet potatoes are black beans' best friend. We don't know why they get along so well, but it's true. They go on all kinds of adventures together in our kitchen, from spicy chili to comforting enchiladas and, of course, nachos. We punch up this irresistible combo with a packet of ranch seasoning. This is such a fun dish to share, but on the off chance that you have some leftovers, add a fried egg on top and have nachos for breakfast.

ONE POT

PREP TIME: 15 MINUTES

COOK TIME: 30 MINUTES

SMART SHOPPING:

We love bean chips in lieu of corn chips. Either the pinto bean or black bean flavor will work well for this dish, but if you want even more spice, try nacho- or pico de gallo–seasoned bean chips.

1 medium sweet potato, peeled and diced
1 tablespoon olive oil
1 (0.9-ounce) package ranch seasoning, divided
1 (5½-ounce) bag tortilla chips or bean chips
1 (15-ounce) can black beans, drained
1 (15½-ounce) jar salsa
1½ cups shredded Cheddar cheese
1 ripe avocado, pitted, peeled, and diced
2 scallions, green and white parts, sliced
¼ cup chopped fresh cilantro
½ cup sour cream
1 lime, quartered

1. Preheat the oven to 350°F. Line a sheet pan with parchment paper.
2. On the prepared sheet pan, toss together the sweet potato, oil, and half of the ranch seasoning, then spread out the mixture into a single layer.
3. Transfer the sheet pan to the oven and bake for 20 minutes, or until the sweet potato has browned around the edges. Remove from the oven.
4. On the same sheet pan, arrange the chips in a single layer, followed by the sweet potato, then the beans.

5. Sprinkle the remaining ranch seasoning over the beans.
6. Add the salsa and cheese. Return the sheet pan to the oven and bake for 10 minutes, or until all the cheese has melted and the nachos are warmed through. Remove from the oven.
7. Garnish with the avocado, scallions, and cilantro.
8. Serve the nachos warm with the sour cream and lime wedges on the side.

ADD IT:
Rice plus beans equals a complete protein, and believe it or not, a cup of cooked rice is really nice added on top of these nachos.

PER SERVING:
CALORIES: 1,359;
FAT: 75G; PROTEIN: 41G;
CARBOHYDRATES: 128G;
FIBER: 31G; SODIUM: 3,977MG

Loaded Mac and Cheese Bowl

Zhuzh up your mac and cheese a little—you know, add some pizzazz! Why eat just a lonely bowl of noodles for supper when you could just as easily top it with flavor-packed mushrooms, tomatoes, and broccoli? It goes from sad to rad, and you add some good nutrition, too.

30 MINUTES OR LESS

PREP TIME: 10 MINUTES

COOK TIME: 15 MINUTES

SMART SHOPPING:
There are plenty of quality brands for vegan and gluten-free mac and cheese these days, including Daiya and Annie's Homegrown.

PER SERVING:
CALORIES: 710;
FAT: 44G; PROTEIN: 32G;
CARBOHYDRATES: 50G;
FIBER: 6G; SODIUM: 1,816MG

1 (10½-ounce) box mac and cheese
1 tablespoon olive oil
2 cups broccoli florets
1 large portobello mushroom, diced
1 pint cherry tomatoes, halved
4 large garlic cloves, sliced
½ teaspoon kosher salt
¼ teaspoon black pepper
4 dashes Tabasco hot sauce

1. Prepare the mac and cheese according to the package instructions. Cover and keep warm.
2. Heat a 12-inch skillet over high heat.
3. Pour in the oil and add the broccoli, mushroom, tomatoes, garlic, salt, pepper, and hot sauce. Cook, stirring often, for 5 minutes. Remove from the heat.
4. Divide the mac and cheese and the broccoli mixture between 2 bowls. Serve warm.

Baked Cincinnati Chili

Chili and spaghetti noodles may seem a bit curious to anyone outside the Midwest, but once you've tried this seemingly odd combination, you'll crave it again and again. Cincinnati chili is usually meat chili served on top of cooked noodles, but we take a different approach, cooking the noodles in vegetarian chili so that they soak up all that good flavor. It's a new, simple, and satisfying way to enjoy an old staple.

8 ounces spaghetti, broken into thirds
1 (15-ounce) can pinto beans
1 (14½-ounce) can diced tomatoes
1 shallot, diced
1 canned chipotle pepper in adobo sauce, minced
1 (8-ounce) package mushrooms, smashed down using your hands
¾ cup water
1 teaspoon kosher salt
½ teaspoon black pepper
1 teaspoon ground cumin
1 tablespoon apple cider vinegar
1 tablespoon olive oil
½ cup shredded Cheddar cheese
Hot sauce, for serving

1. Preheat the oven to 400°F.
2. In a medium casserole dish, combine the spaghetti, beans, tomatoes, shallot, chipotle pepper, mushrooms, water, salt, pepper, cumin, vinegar, and oil. Stir to combine. Cover and bake for 30 minutes. Remove from the oven.
3. Uncover, stir, top with the cheese, and return to the oven for another 25 minutes. Remove from the oven. Serve warm with hot sauce on the side.

ONE POT

PREP TIME: 10 MINUTES
COOK TIME: 55 MINUTES

ADD IT:
Anything worth eating is worth adding hot sauce to, especially anything chili related. We have at least seven kinds of hot sauce in our refrigerator at all times. We're all about flavor, not just heat, and a little hot sauce goes a long way in that department.

PER SERVING:
CALORIES: 858;
FAT: 19G; PROTEIN: 36G;
CARBOHYDRATES: 136G;
FIBER: 16G; SODIUM: 1,691MG

Skillet Pot Pie

Making pot pie the traditional way can be time intensive: roll out the crust, blind-bake it, etc. Look, it's a weeknight, and we have stuff to do and shows to watch, so we devised this one-skillet pot pie with a crispy biscuit topping.

PREP TIME: 15 MINUTES

COOK TIME: 35 MINUTES

SWAP IT:

Try veggie turkey slices (such as Tofurky brand) in place of the tofu here for a fairly realistic turkey pot pie experience. Trust us, it's good!

PER SERVING:
CALORIES: 695;
FAT: 31G; PROTEIN: 29G;
CARBOHYDRATES: 77G;
FIBER: 4G; SODIUM: 1,887MG

1 (6-ounce) can biscuits
1 tablespoon unsalted butter
1 tablespoon all-purpose flour
2 cups whole milk
1 large shallot, diced
1 medium carrot, diced
1 medium celery stalk, diced
1 medium Yukon Gold potato, diced
1 (6-ounce) package baked tofu, diced
1 teaspoon dried thyme
1 vegetarian bouillon cube
½ teaspoon black pepper

1. Preheat the oven to 350°F.
2. Bake the biscuits according to the package instructions, then split them.
3. In a small oven-safe skillet, melt the butter over medium-high heat.
4. Add the flour and whisk until nutty and fragrant.
5. Add the milk and whisk until smooth.
6. Add the shallot, carrot, celery, potato, tofu, thyme, bouillon cube, and pepper. Stir. Cook for 3 to 5 minutes, or until the mixture just starts to bubble.
7. Add the biscuits, cut-side down, on top. Remove from the heat.
8. Transfer the skillet to the oven and bake for 12 to 15 minutes, or until the biscuits are deep golden brown. Remove from the oven. Serve warm.

Tofu Dumplings

You may think making pasta from scratch takes too much effort—until you try this recipe! These little dumplings require no special tools, skills, or pasta-making experience. So take a break from the typical box of dried noodles and give these protein-packed pasta pillows a chance to shine.

1 (14-ounce) package extra-firm tofu, drained and crumbled
Grated zest and juice of 1 lemon
½ teaspoon kosher salt, plus more for the water
1 teaspoon olive oil
1½ cups all-purpose flour, divided
1 (6.35-ounce) jar pesto

1. In a large bowl, combine the tofu, lemon zest, lemon juice, salt, oil, and 1¼ cups of flour. Knead until a dough just forms. Just be sure not to overwork it.
2. Fill an 8-quart stockpot with water, salt it, and place it over high heat. Bring to a gentle boil.
3. Lightly flour a cutting board with the remaining ¼ cup of flour. On the board, pat the dough out flat until it's ¼ inch thick and roughly 8 by 10 inches.
4. Using a pizza wheel or floured knife, cut the dough into 1-inch squares.
5. Push the dumplings into the gently boiling water and cook for 1 to 2 minutes, or until they float. Remove from the heat.
6. Divide the dumplings between 2 bowls.
7. Top each bowl with half of the pesto. Serve warm.

5-INGREDIENT
30 MINUTES OR LESS
ONE POT

PREP TIME: 10 MINUTES
COOK TIME: 5 MINUTES

SWAP IT:
We suggest using pesto sauce here, but these dumplings are terrific with sautéed cabbage or with marinara, or you can even keep it simple with a little black pepper, garlic, olive oil, and Romano cheese.

PER SERVING:
CALORIES: 863;
FAT: 46G; PROTEIN: 33G;
CARBOHYDRATES: 77G;
FIBER: 7G; SODIUM: 1,215MG

Vegan Fondue

Fondue without the cheese? What a world we live in. I mean, who could have imagined that it was even possible? The thing is, it's not only possible—it's fantastic! There are so many good dairy alternatives available these days, and this recipe is a go-to appetizer that vegan or lactose-intolerant folks will happily enjoy. We use an easy roux here in the cooking process to make sure the sauce stands up to your dippers.

PREP TIME: 15 MINUTES

COOK TIME: 20 MINUTES

SMART SHOPPING:

Any shredded cheese, even if it's not mozzarella, can be substituted here. The color of the final result will be different, but the taste will be pretty similar. If you're looking for a dairy-free fondue, Daiya and Follow Your Heart brands make excellent products.

1 cup cubed French bread
1 cup broccoli florets
1 cup baby potatoes, halved
1 red bell pepper, sliced
1 tablespoon olive oil
1 tablespoon all-purpose flour
½ cup white wine, such as pinot grigio
Juice of 1 lemon
2 garlic cloves, minced
1 tablespoon Dijon mustard
⅛ teaspoon grated nutmeg
1 (7.1-ounce) package vegan mozzarella shreds
Up to ½ cup water, for thinning
1 cup halved cherry tomatoes

1. Preheat the oven to 400°F. Line a sheet pan with parchment paper.
2. Put the bread, broccoli, potatoes, and bell pepper on the prepared sheet pan.
3. Transfer the sheet pan to the oven and cook for 20 minutes, or until the potatoes are soft and cooked through. Remove from the oven.
4. Meanwhile, heat a medium saucepan over medium heat.
5. Pour in the oil and add the flour. Whisk until the flour becomes nutty and fragrant.

6. Add the wine and whisk until there are no lumps.
7. Add the lemon juice, garlic, mustard, nutmeg, and vegan mozzarella. Whisk until the mozzarella has melted.
8. Add water to thin the mixture to a pancake batter–like consistency. Remove from the heat.
9. Serve the fondue in a bowl with the bread, roasted vegetables, and tomatoes arranged around it.

USE IT UP:
Dijon mustard is something we always have in the refrigerator. Add a teaspoon of it to homemade salad dressing for an extra kick, put it on your morning Black-Eyed Pea Sausages (page 29) and biscuits, and dip your pretzels in it for a snack.

PER SERVING:
CALORIES: 557;
FAT: 33G; PROTEIN: 10G;
CARBOHYDRATES: 50G;
FIBER: 9G; SODIUM: 732MG

Cabbage Roll Casserole

Many cultures have their own version of cabbage rolls. Ours take a pretty traditional eastern European route with two exceptions: they're plant-based, and we don't roll them up. We stack the filling and cabbage leaves more like a lasagna.

PREP TIME: 10 MINUTES

COOK TIME: 45 MINUTES

SWAP IT:
Instant rice works fine in this recipe if you're looking to save some time.

PER SERVING:
CALORIES: 730;
FAT: 13G; PROTEIN: 40G;
CARBOHYDRATES: 107G;
FIBER:23G;SODIUM:3,377MG

1 small head cabbage
1 tablespoon olive oil, plus 2 teaspoons
1 medium onion, finely diced
½ cup white wine
1½ cups plant-based crumbles
1 cup cooked rice
4 cups tomato sauce, divided
½ cup bread crumbs

1. Preheat the oven to 350°F.
2. Cover the cabbage with a paper towel and microwave for 7 minutes. Let cool.
3. Once the cabbage has cooled, run your knife around the core, and the leaves will pull apart.
4. Heat a medium pan over medium-high heat.
5. Pour in 1 tablespoon of oil and add the onion. Cook for 5 minutes, or until the onion begins to brown. Add the wine and cook until most of it has evaporated. Add the crumbles and rice. Turn off the heat.
6. In a 6-by-9-inch casserole dish, combine 2 cups of tomato sauce and 4 large cabbage leaves overlapping.
7. Add the rice mixture and top with more cabbage leaves, the remaining 2 cups of tomato sauce, and the bread crumbs.
8. Drizzle the top with the remaining 2 teaspoons of oil. Transfer the dish to the oven and bake for 30 minutes. Serve warm.

Quiche Lawrence

Amy loved this quiche so much the first time we made it, we went ahead and named it after her. It uses mushrooms to mimic the flavor and texture of bacon. When you are tasked with cooking for vegetarians, this should be your go-to recipe.

1 tablespoon toasted sesame oil
1 (8-ounce) package sliced mushrooms
1 medium shallot, diced
1 cup Greek yogurt
2 large eggs, beaten
½ cup shredded smoked Gouda cheese
1 tablespoon maple syrup
1 teaspoon kosher salt
½ teaspoon black pepper
1 prepared piecrust

1. Preheat the oven to 350°F.
2. Heat a medium skillet over high heat.
3. Pour in the oil and add the mushrooms. Cook for 5 minutes, or until the mushrooms start to brown. Remove from the heat.
4. Stir in the shallot.
5. In a large bowl, combine the mushroom mixture, yogurt, eggs, cheese, maple syrup, salt, and pepper. Pour into the piecrust.
6. Transfer the piecrust to the oven and bake for 30 to 35 minutes, or until the center of the quiche puffs up slightly. Remove from the oven. Serve warm or at room temperature.

PREP TIME: 10 MINUTES

COOK TIME: 40 MINUTES

SMART SHOPPING:
We often buy gluten-free piecrust (such as Wholly Wholesome brand) in order to have that option on hand for those who follow that diet.

PER SERVING:
CALORIES: 854;
FAT: 52G; PROTEIN: 32G;
CARBOHYDRATES: 73G;
FIBER:1.5G;SODIUM:1,480MG

Beans and Baby Carrot Franks

This meatless take on beans and franks completely transforms a ho-hum bag of baby carrots. It's sweet, savory, and a good bit healthier than the original.

ONE POT

MINIMAL PREP

PREP TIME: 5 MINUTES

COOK TIME: 30 MINUTES

PAIR IT:

Make a simple slaw by adding mayonnaise, scallions, mustard, salt, and pepper to shredded cabbage. It'll make a nice topping and add some veggie crunch to this dish.

PER SERVING:
CALORIES: 563;
FAT: 18G; PROTEIN: 18G;
CARBOHYDRATES: 81G;
FIBER: 16G; SODIUM: 1,906MG

1 tablespoon sesame oil
1 small onion, diced
1 (1-pound) package baby carrots
1 (16-ounce) can vegetarian baked beans
1 canned chipotle pepper in adobo sauce, minced
¾ cup water
1 tablespoon Dijon mustard
1 tablespoon soy sauce
¼ cup ketchup
½ teaspoon black pepper
½ cup shredded Cheddar cheese

1. Heat a medium saucepan over high heat.
2. Pour in the oil and add the onion. Cook for 5 minutes, or until browned.
3. Add the carrots, beans with their liquid, chipotle pepper, water, mustard, soy sauce, ketchup, and black pepper. Bring to a boil.
4. Reduce the heat to a simmer. Cover the saucepan and cook for 20 minutes, or until the carrots are soft. Remove from the heat.
5. Sprinkle the cheese on top and serve warm.

Brussels Sprouts and Apples

The leaves are rustling in the cool wind, a fire is in the fireplace, and the days are getting shorter. Let's put wonderful fall ingredients to use in this one-skillet wonder with a lovely balance of earthy and sweet notes. Now, where did I put my favorite sweater?

1 pound Brussels sprouts, halved
1 medium onion, diced
1 medium Pink Lady or Honeycrisp apple, cored and diced
2 tablespoons mustard
1 tablespoon soy sauce
1 tablespoon maple syrup
1 tablespoon olive oil
2 plant-based sausages

1. Preheat the oven to 400°F.
2. In a large bowl, combine the Brussels sprouts, onion, apple, mustard, soy sauce, maple syrup, and oil. Stir to coat.
3. Heat a medium skillet over medium-high heat.
4. Put the sausages in the skillet and cook for 3 minutes.
5. Turn the sausages and add the Brussels sprouts mixture. Cook for 25 minutes, or until the edges of the Brussels sprouts are slightly brown. Remove from the heat. Serve warm.

PREP TIME: 10 MINUTES

COOK TIME: 30 MINUTES

SWAP IT:
We love using plant-based sausages, such as Beyond Meat brand, in this recipe, but swapping in a couple of portobello mushrooms would be just as delish.

PER SERVING:
CALORIES: 445;
FAT: 19G; PROTEIN: 24G;
CARBOHYDRATES: 46G;
FIBER: 14G; SODIUM: 1,354MG

Green Goddess Grain Bowl

This is a recipe, sure, but it's also an idea that could make for an endless array of recipes for breakfast, lunch, or dinner. It's as versatile as it is delicious. The idea is that if you top grains with beans, greens, tomatoes, a delicious dressing, and some nuts or seeds, then you've got yourself some good, healthy fuel.

30 MINUTES OR LESS

PREP TIME: 15 MINUTES

COOK TIME: 5 MINUTES

SWAP IT:
This could easily be a couscous bowl topped with spinach, chickpeas, and almonds.

PER SERVING:
CALORIES: 1,150;
FAT: 61G; PROTEIN: 36G;
CARBOHYDRATES: 128G;
FIBER: 38G; SODIUM: 1,424MG

1 tablespoon olive oil
1 cup diced onion (about 1 small)
1 bunch greens, such as lacinato kale, chopped
Juice of 2 medium lemons, divided
1 (15-ounce) can beans, such as black beans
2 medium ripe avocados, pitted and peeled
1 teaspoon honey
2 scallions, green and white parts, sliced
¼ cup mayonnaise
1 tablespoon sriracha
2 cups cooked grains, such as quinoa or wild rice
¼ cup sunflower seeds

1. Heat a 12-inch pan over medium-high heat.
2. Pour in the oil and add the onion. Cook for 5 minutes, or until lightly browned.
3. Add the greens, juice of 1 lemon, and the beans. Cover the pan. Remove from the heat.
4. To make the dressing, in a medium bowl, mash the avocados with the juice of the remaining lemon, the honey, scallions, mayonnaise, and sriracha.
5. Build bowls with the grains topped with the bean mixture, dressing, and sunflower seeds.

Sheet Pan Stir-Fry with Peanut Sauce

Twice a week . . . easily. That's how often we make this dish. It's so versatile and simple that it works perfectly for lunch or dinner. The key is the two-ingredient sauce made with smooth peanut butter and sriracha. As for the mixed vegetables, use any combination, such as scallions, carrots, broccoli, bell pepper, bok choy, cabbage, celery, or cauliflower.

6 cups mixed vegetables, chopped
1 tablespoon soy sauce
1 tablespoon toasted sesame oil
¼ cup smooth peanut butter
¼ cup water
1 tablespoon sriracha
2 cups cooked rice
¼ cup chopped peanuts

1. Preheat the oven to 400°F. Line a sheet pan with parchment paper.
2. On the prepared sheet pan, combine the mixed vegetables, soy sauce, and oil.
3. Transfer the sheet pan to the oven and cook for 20 minutes. Remove from the oven.
4. To make the sauce, in a medium bowl, whisk together the peanut butter, water, and sriracha.
5. Serve the rice topped with the vegetables, peanuts, and plenty of sauce.

PREP TIME: 20 MINUTES

COOK TIME: 20 MINUTES

USE IT UP:
We think of this recipe as our "clear the refrigerator" stir-fry. Sometimes we'll chop up most of the vegetables in the refrigerator and save half of them in a container for the next recipe, like a veggie frittata or roasted vegetable tomato sauce.

PER SERVING:
CALORIES: 898;
FAT: 35G; PROTEIN: 27G;
CARBOHYDRATES: 120G;
FIBER: 15G; SODIUM: 894MG

Baked Eggplant Schnitzel

We use eggplant to create our take on this German dish. Smashed-up pretzels add crunch to the dish and mean you won't need to do any messy pan-frying.

PREP TIME: 15 MINUTES

COOK TIME: 20 MINUTES

PAIR IT:

Roast some baby potatoes in olive oil and sprinkle on a little salt for a side dish that will round out the meal.

PER SERVING:
CALORIES: 422;
FAT: 9.5G; PROTEIN: 7G;
CARBOHYDRATES: 68G;
FIBER: 8G; SODIUM: 2,117MG

1 cup pretzels
¼ cup Dijon mustard
1 tablespoon maple syrup
1 medium eggplant, cut lengthwise
  into 4 (½-inch-thick) pieces
1 tablespoon olive oil
Black pepper
1 cup sauerkraut
1 lemon, quartered

1. Preheat the oven to 375°F. Line a sheet pan with parchment paper.
2. To make pretzel crumbs, put your favorite pretzels or pretzel sticks in a food processor and process, or just place the pretzels in a plastic bag and crush them using a rolling pin.
3. In a medium bowl, combine the mustard and maple syrup. Using a silicone brush or a spoon, coat both sides of each of the eggplant slices with the mustard mixture.
4. Dredge the eggplant in the pretzel crumbs, pressing each slice into the crumbs to coat.
5. Put the eggplant on the prepared sheet pan. Drizzle with the oil and season with pepper.
6. Transfer the sheet pan to the oven and bake for 20 minutes, or until the eggplant is crunchy on the outside and soft and pliable on the inside. Remove from the oven. Serve warm with the sauerkraut and lemon wedges.

RICE

When we cook rice, we always make extra. It's awesome to have it ready to be used at a moment's notice without the 30-minute wait time. We keep two servings of cooked rice in a container in the freezer, but because there's always a chance we need some rice *stat*, we've come to love stashing two boxes of instant rice, white and brown, in the cupboard.

So once you're ready to use up your cooked rice, take a look at Cabbage Roll Casserole (page 104) or Breakfast Fried Rice (page 21). You also may use it as a base in Green Goddess Grain Bowl (page 108) or Sheet Pan Stir-Fry with Peanut Sauce (page 109). Plenty of recipes in this book call for rice, so having some cooked, frozen rice on hand lets you get the jump on a recipe.

For a savory snack, heat up 1 cup rice, and top with 1 tablespoon kimchi and 2 tablespoons chopped peanuts.

We also never turn down a bowl of 1 cup warm rice with 1 tablespoon butter, ½ tablespoon soy sauce or mirin, a pinch of sugar, and 1 teaspoon sambal oelek.

We love to take 1 cup rice and top it with 1 diced peeled mango and 1 tablespoon honey for a quick dessert.

Blueberry Cobbler with Corn Bread Topping
PAGE 120

chapter 6

DESSERTS

Cashew Cheesecake

Cheesecake is always a good bet! The cashews we use in this recipe add even more protein to the mix.

PREP TIME: 20 MINUTES, PLUS AT LEAST 4 HOURS TO SET

COOK TIME: 1 HOUR

ADD IT:

Strawberries, raspberries, or blueberries on the side or a generous drizzle of melted chocolate would make wonderful accompaniments to this cheesecake.

PER SERVING (1 SLICE):
CALORIES: 581;
FAT: 38G; PROTEIN: 10G;
CARBOHYDRATES: 51G;
FIBER: 1.5G; SODIUM: 749MG

4 ounces graham crackers (about 6 sheets)
3 tablespoons unsalted butter
¼ cup plus 2 tablespoons sugar
1¼ teaspoons, divided kosher salt
1 (8-ounce) container cream cheese, at room temperature
1 (6-ounce) container plain whole-milk yogurt
½ cup raw unsalted cashews
2 teaspoons vanilla extract

1. Preheat the oven to 350°F.
2. Put the graham crackers in a plastic bag. Using a rolling pin, crush them. Transfer to a medium bowl.
3. In a small microwave-safe bowl, microwave the butter for 30 seconds, or until melted.
4. Using a silicone brush, coat the bottom and sides of a 6-inch round springform pan with some of the melted butter.
5. To make the crust, combine the remaining butter with the graham cracker crumbs, sugar, and ¼ teaspoon of salt. Mix until incorporated.
6. Press the crust into the bottom of the prepared springform pan.
7. To make the filling, in a food processor, combine the cream cheese, yogurt, cashews, vanilla, and remaining 1 tablespoon of salt. Blend until smooth.
8. Pour the filling into the crust and smooth with a spatula.

9. Transfer the pan to the oven and bake for 1 hour, or until the cheesecake has lightly browned on top. Remove from the oven.
10. Set the cheesecake on the counter to cool and then place it in the refrigerator for at least 4 hours or overnight to set.
11. Remove the cheesecake from the pan, slice into 4 pieces, and serve.

Strawberry-Balsamic Crisp

Strawberry and balsamic vinegar are two familiar flavors that you may not always think of together, but they complement each other because the verdant notes of the strawberries are offset by the deep, sweet tanginess of the vinegar. We use black pepper in this combo to spice it up and add yet another layer of flavor.

PREP TIME: 20 MINUTES

COOK TIME: 1 HOUR

SMART SHOPPING:

We always have organic, unbleached all-purpose flour on hand for baking, but it's nice to have some other options available to modify recipes for different diets and preferences if needed. Rye flour especially works well in this recipe and adds more flavor to the topping.

PER SERVING:
CALORIES: 968;
FAT: 48G; PROTEIN: 10G;
CARBOHYDRATES: 132G;
FIBER: 11G; SODIUM: 579MG

4 cups fresh or frozen strawberries, chopped
Juice of 1 lemon
Juice of 1 orange
1 tablespoon raspberry jam
2 tablespoons granulated sugar
½ teaspoon kosher salt
1 tablespoon balsamic vinegar
3 tablespoons unsalted butter, divided
1 tablespoon all-purpose flour, plus ½ cup
1 tablespoon light brown sugar, plus ¼ cup packed
¾ cup rolled oats
¼ cup olive oil
½ teaspoon kosher salt
½ teaspoon black pepper

1. Preheat the oven to 400°F.
2. In a medium baking dish, combine the strawberries, lemon juice, orange juice, jam, granulated sugar, salt, vinegar, 1 tablespoon of butter, 1 tablespoon of flour, and 1 tablespoon of brown sugar. Mix until the berries are coated.
3. Transfer the baking dish to the oven and bake for 30 minutes.

4. Meanwhile, make the topping: Coarsely chop the remaining 2 tablespoons of butter. Transfer to a bowl and combine with the remaining ½ cup of flour, ¼ cup of brown sugar, the oats, oil, salt, and pepper.

5. Once the strawberries have baked for 30 minutes, add the topping. Bake for another 30 minutes, or until the filling is bubbling and the topping has browned. Remove from the oven. Let cool. Serve warm.

Brandied Fruit

We make this caramelized skillet of mixed fruit just about every week; it is in heavy rotation for a good reason. It is one of those recipes we've depended on for so long for pie filling and apple crisp, as a wonderful topping for ice cream, or just for enjoying on its own. The key to this dish is to stir it every few minutes while you watch for the liquid to evaporate, concentrating the flavors and creating a syrupy and caramelized treat. If you would like to make a brandied fruit pie, we've got you covered—our easy olive oil piecrust recipe is included.

ONE POT

PREP TIME:
15 MINUTES, PLUS
1 HOUR 10 MINUTES IF
MAKING THE PIE

COOK TIME:
30 MINUTES, PLUS
20 MINUTES IF
MAKING THE PIE

USE IT UP:

We find golden raisins to be softer in texture and more flavorful than the usual ones we all grew up either enjoying or lamenting. Use golden raisins in curries, trail mix, and smoothies for a pop of sweet, juicy flavor.

For the brandied fruit:

8 small or 4 large pears or apples,
  peeled and coarsely chopped
Juice of 1 lemon
2 tablespoons honey
2 tablespoons brown sugar
¼ cup water
¼ cup brandy
½ teaspoon vanilla extract
⅓ cup dried cherries
⅓ cup golden raisins
1 teaspoon cornstarch, sifted
¼ teaspoon kosher salt
½ teaspoon pumpkin pie spice
1 tablespoon unsalted butter

For the piecrust (optional):

1 cup all-purpose flour, plus more for dusting
¼ teaspoon kosher salt
¼ cup olive oil
About ¼ cup ice water

To make the brandied fruit:

In a medium skillet, combine the pears, lemon juice, honey, sugar, water, brandy, vanilla, dried cherries, raisins, cornstarch, salt, pumpkin pie spice, and butter. Cook over medium heat, stirring every 3 minutes, for 20 to 30 minutes, or until the mixture caramelizes and reduces by about a third. Remove from the heat. Serve warm.

To make the piecrust (optional):

1. Preheat the oven to 350°F.
2. In a mixing bowl, combine the flour and salt.
3. Add the oil and mix until a rough dough forms.
4. Add the water, 1 teaspoon at a time, mixing after each addition, until the ingredients are incorporated and a dough ball is formed.
5. Cover the bowl and let the dough rest in the refrigerator for 1 hour.
6. Lightly flour the work surface and the dough. Roll out the dough into a circle large enough to fit your pie pan.
7. Press the dough into the pie pan.
8. Spoon the brandied bruit into the piecrust.
9. Transfer the pie pan to the oven and bake for 15 to 20 minutes, or until the piecrust has lightly browned. Remove from the oven. Cut into 6 wedges.

ADD IT:
This is such a versatile recipe! It makes for an excellent breakfast, especially if you top it with the oat mixture we use on page 116 for Strawberry-Balsamic Crisp. Use it as a topping for vanilla ice cream or your favorite granola; serve it with whipped cream or Greek yogurt on top for breakfast; or try our new favorite thing: spoon the baked fruit into the folds of prepared cinnamon rolls before baking them.

PER SERVING (FRUIT ONLY):
CALORIES: 651;
FAT: 6.5G; PROTEIN: 3G;
CARBOHYDRATES: 144G;
FIBER: 17G; SODIUM: 157MG

PER SERVING (1 WEDGE OF PIE):
CALORIES: 372;
FAT: 11G; PROTEIN: 3G;
CARBOHYDRATES: 64G;
FIBER: 6G; SODIUM: 100MG

Blueberry Cobbler with Corn Bread Topping

Y'all must know that Southerners like us have figured out how to have corn bread for dessert. For this recipe, we pour a simple buttermilk corn bread mixture over some fresh blueberries, and—be still our hearts—it's heaven on earth.

PREP TIME: 15 MINUTES

COOK TIME: 25 MINUTES

USE IT UP:

You'll have some buttermilk left over after you make this recipe, but don't despair—you can use it in pancakes, in biscuits, or for your French toast. If you don't have buttermilk on hand, you can make your own by adding 2 teaspoons distilled white vinegar to ¾ cup milk and wait for 5 minutes before using it.

1 pint blueberries

¾ teaspoon kosher salt, divided

3 tablespoons unsalted butter, cut into small cubes, divided

¼ cup sugar

Grated zest of and juice of 1 lemon

1 tablespoon all-purpose flour, plus 1½ cups

½ cup cornmeal

¾ cup buttermilk

1 teaspoon baking powder

1 large egg

2 scoops vanilla gelato or 1 cup whipped cream (optional)

1. Preheat the oven to 400°F.
2. Put the blueberries, ½ teaspoon of salt, 1 tablespoon of butter, the sugar, lemon zest, lemon juice, and 1 tablespoon of flour in a small oven-safe skillet. Toss to combine.
3. To make the topping, in a medium bowl, combine the remaining 1½ cups of flour, the cornmeal, remaining ¼ teaspoon of salt, remaining 2 tablespoons of butter, the buttermilk, baking powder, and egg. Mix together.

4. Spoon the topping onto the blueberry mixture and spread it around until it covers most of the blueberry layer, leaving some openings.
5. Transfer the skillet to the oven and bake for 25 minutes, or until the blueberry mixture is bubbling and the corn bread topping appears golden brown. Remove from the oven.
6. Serve the cobbler warm with the gelato (if using).

PER SERVING:
CALORIES: 924;
FAT: 24G; PROTEIN: 21G;
CARBOHYDRATES: 158G;
FIBER: 8G; SODIUM: 561MG

Spiked Hot Cocoa Tiramisu

Tiramisu is very easy to put together, but it looks like quite an impressive dessert. This recipe changes it up a bit with a boozy twist on hot chocolate, and it even utilizes hot chocolate mix in the layers. It's a good idea to plan to prepare this dessert a day ahead of time to allow the flavors to meld and the ladyfingers to soften up overnight.

PREP TIME: 20 MINUTES, PLUS AT LEAST 5 HOURS TO CHILL

SWAP IT:

Feel free to use cream cheese in place of the mascarpone cheese if that is what you have readily available. Using Neufchâtel cheese in place of the mascarpone and subbing in low-fat whipping cream, such as Truwhip whipped topping, will lower this recipe's fat content.

For the homemade whipped cream (if not using store-bought):

¾ cup heavy cream
1 tablespoon sugar
½ teaspoon vanilla extract
⅛ teaspoon kosher salt

For the tiramisu:

1 cup whipped cream, store-bought or homemade
½ cup mascarpone cheese
¼ cup maple syrup
¼ teaspoon kosher salt
½ cup strong brewed coffee
¼ cup bourbon
12 ladyfinger cakes
1 tablespoon hot cocoa mix, divided
¼ cup mini dark chocolate chips
½ cup mini marshmallows (optional)

To make the homemade whipped cream (optional):

1. Pour the cream into a tall bowl. While tipping the bowl slightly in order to incorporate the maximum amount of air into the cream, whisk in a steady, circular motion for 1 minute.
2. Add the sugar and whisk for about 1 minute, or until incorporated.

3. Add the vanilla and salt. Whisk until incorporated.
4. Store the whipped cream in an airtight container in the refrigerator until ready to use.

To make the tiramisu:

1. In a medium bowl, whisk together the whipped cream, cheese, maple syrup, and salt for about 2 minutes, or until smooth.
2. In another bowl, combine the coffee and bourbon.
3. In a 5-by-9-inch loaf pan, spread one-third of the cheese and whipped cream mixture to begin the tiramisu.
4. Cut about an inch off each of the ladyfingers so that they will fit snugly in the loaf pan. Crumble the trimmings and reserve.
5. One at a time, quickly dip 6 ladyfingers in the coffee and bourbon mixture. Add them in 1 layer to the loaf pan.
6. Top the ladyfinger layer with one-third of the cheese and whipped cream mixture and sprinkle ½ tablespoon of hot cocoa mix on top.
7. Repeat the layers once again: coffee-and-bourbon-dipped ladyfingers, one-third of the cheese and whipped cream mixture, and the remaining ½ tablespoon of hot cocoa mix on top.
8. Sprinkle the top of the tiramisu with mini dark chocolate chips, reserved crumbled ladyfingers, and mini marshmallows (if using).
9. Put the loaf pan in the refrigerator for at least 5 hours or overnight.

SMART SHOPPING:
When shopping for staples like vanilla, it's good to splurge just a little bit. Look for "pure vanilla extract" printed on the bottle.

PER SERVING (½ CUP WHIPPED CREAM):
CALORIES: 222; FAT: 22G; PROTEIN: 2G; CARBOHYDRATES: 6G; FIBER: 0G; SODIUM: 63MG

PER SERVING (TIRAMISU):
CALORIES: 904; FAT: 44G; PROTEIN: 14G; CARBOHYDRATES: 95G; FIBER: 2.5G; SODIUM: 339MG

Date and Peanut Turtles

These taste like one of our favorite candy bars—minus the sugar high and inevitable crash. Double or triple this recipe to share with your friends or to wrap up a box of these as a gift.

5-INGREDIENT
MINIMAL PREP

PREP TIME: 5 MINUTES, PLUS AT LEAST 1 HOUR TO CHILL

COOK TIME: 1 MINUTE

SMART SHOPPING:

You want nice, soft dried dates for this. Look for ones that are dark in color. If the dates you have aren't very pliable, microwave them for 20 seconds with 1 teaspoon water, drain off the water, and move forward with the recipe.

PER SERVING:
CALORIES: 300;
FAT: 21G; PROTEIN: 8G;
CARBOHYDRATES: 33G;
FIBER: 7G; SODIUM: 81MG

¼ cup chopped pitted dates (about 3 large dates)
¼ cup chopped peanuts
1½ ounces stevia-sweetened dark chocolate (about ½ bar)
⅛ teaspoon kosher salt

1. Line a plate with parchment paper.
2. In a small bowl, mix together the dates and peanuts well.
3. Divide the mixture into 4 spheres. Put them on the prepared plate.
4. Using your hand, lightly flatten the spheres into disks.
5. Put the chocolate in a small microwave-safe bowl. Microwave for 30 seconds. Stir, then microwave for 15 seconds, and stir again.
6. Using a spoon, drizzle the chocolate over the disks.
7. Garnish with the salt and refrigerate for at least 1 hour to allow the chocolate to harden.

Carrot Cake Truffles

What's better than sneaking a root vegetable into your dessert, especially when it tastes this good? These no-bake, refined sugar–free truffles come together in a snap and will be gone just as quickly.

¼ cup finely grated carrot (about 1 small)
½ cup cream cheese, at room temperature
¼ cup golden raisins
½ teaspoon pumpkin pie spice
1 tablespoon maple syrup
½ cup quick-cooking oats
⅛ teaspoon kosher salt
¼ cup finely chopped walnuts

1. In a medium bowl, combine the carrot, cream cheese, raisins, pumpkin pie spice, maple syrup, oats, and salt. Stir until well incorporated. Refrigerate for 10 minutes.
2. Using a mini ice cream scoop or tablespoon, scoop the mixture and drop it into the walnuts. Roll to lightly coat. Repeat until all of the mixture has been used. It should make about 10 truffles.
3. Chill the truffles on a plate in the refrigerator for at least 1 hour before serving.

ONE POT

PREP TIME: 10 MINUTES, PLUS AT LEAST 1 HOUR TO CHILL

SWAP IT:

Use vegan cream cheese by brands like Tofutti or Daiya to make these little beauties dairy-free.

PER SERVING:
CALORIES: 468;
FAT: 31G; PROTEIN: 9G;
CARBOHYDRATES: 43G;
FIBER: 4G; SODIUM: 266MG

Grilled S'mores Sandwich

This is modeled on a grilled cheese sandwich, but, and here's the kicker, it features chocolate and marshmallows inside instead of cheese. We know—it's devilish to even put such ideas in your head, but we've gone and done it. One sandwich cut in half is the perfect amount for two people.

5-INGREDIENT

30 MINUTES OR LESS

ONE POT

MINIMAL PREP

PREP TIME: 5 MINUTES

COOK TIME: 10 MINUTES

SMART SHOPPING:
Marshmallows typically have gelatin, which is not a vegetarian ingredient. Look for Dandies brand or other vegan or vegetarian marshmallows for this recipe.

PER SERVING:
CALORIES: 312;
FAT: 14G; PROTEIN: 4G;
CARBOHYDRATES: 42G;
FIBER: 3G; SODIUM: 139MG

2 teaspoons unsalted butter, divided
2 slices bread
1½ ounces dark chocolate (about ½ bar)
½ cup mini vegan marshmallows
1 teaspoon honey

1. In a medium skillet, melt 1 teaspoon of butter over medium heat.
2. In the skillet, layer 1 bread slice, the chocolate, marshmallows, and the other bread slice. Cook for 3 minutes.
3. Add the remaining 1 teaspoon of butter to the top piece of bread and flip carefully. Cook for 3 minutes, or until the chocolate is melty and the bread has toasted. Remove from the heat. Let cool for at least 5 minutes.
4. Cut the sandwich in half to share.
5. Drizzle the top of each portion with the honey before serving warm.

Skillet-Baked Brie with Cinnamon Tortilla Chips

Bonsoir! Bonsoir! Over here. We were just about to start the cheese course, and we're so glad you showed up for it. Cheese often appears on the table as a prelude to the dessert course in France. So we bake a wheel of French Brie covered in dried apricots and sliced almonds for this sweet homage to *fromage*.

2 (10-inch) flour tortillas, each cut into 8 pieces
½ teaspoon ground cinnamon
1 teaspoon olive oil
1 (6-ounce) wheel Brie cheese
¼ cup diced dried apricots (about 6 apricots)
¼ cup sliced almonds
2 tablespoons honey

1. Preheat the oven to 350°F. Line a sheet pan with parchment paper.
2. In a medium bowl, toss together the tortillas, cinnamon, and oil until well coated.
3. Lay the tortillas out in a single layer on the prepared sheet pan.
4. Put the cheese in the center of a 10-inch oven-safe skillet and top with the apricots and almonds.
5. Transfer the sheet pan and skillet to the oven and bake for 13 minutes. Remove both the sheet pan and skillet from the oven.
6. Arrange the tortillas around the cheese and drizzle everything with the honey. Serve warm and provide a small cheese knife on the side.

30 MINUTES OR LESS

PREP TIME: 10 MINUTES

COOK TIME: 15 MINUTES

SWAP IT:

French bread would be an even heartier cheese scooper than the tortilla chips featured in this recipe. We also sometimes use apricot jam instead of dried apricots; just add the jam on top of the Brie after baking.

PER SERVING:
CALORIES: 684;
FAT: 37G; PROTEIN: 27G;
CARBOHYDRATES: 66G;
FIBER: 3.5G; SODIUM: 1,167MG

Tangy Peanut Butter and Banana Pudding

This is not pudding with bananas in it, which is sacrosanct in our Southern neck of the woods. This is pudding made from bananas. The texture blends perfectly with peanut butter to yield a silky, smooth dessert that is sugar-free.

5-INGREDIENT
ONE POT

PREP TIME: 10 MINUTES, PLUS AT LEAST 1 HOUR TO CHILL

SWAP IT:

To change it up, use any nut butter you'd like. Cashew butter will be sweeter and smoother, whereas almond butter will have an earthy flavor and a bit more texture.

PER SERVING:
CALORIES: 363;
FAT: 22G; PROTEIN: 10G;
CARBOHYDRATES: 40G;
FIBER: 6G; SODIUM: 208MG

2 medium ripe bananas, peeled
Juice of 1 medium lemon
¼ cup peanut butter
⅛ teaspoon kosher salt
1 tablespoon grated stevia-sweetened dark chocolate
1 tablespoon chopped peanuts

1. In a food processor, combine the bananas, lemon juice, peanut butter, and salt. Blend until very smooth.
2. Divide the mixture between 2 dessert bowls.
3. Garnish with the chocolate and peanuts. Refrigerate for at least 1 hour before serving.

USE IT UP:
MAPLE SYRUP

Maple syrup has so many excellent uses besides happily drowning pancakes and waffles. We try to use an array of natural sweeteners at our house, simply for the sake of variety and flavor. Maple syrup is as sweet as it gets, so it's good to use it in moderation, but it's a little-known fact that it contains quite a few minerals as well as a nice dose of antioxidants.

Make your own fruit syrup for a fancy weekend brunch at home by combining ¼ cup maple syrup with 1 cup chopped berries of your choice, the juice of 1 lemon, and a pinch of kosher salt. Place the mixture in a small saucepan over medium heat, stirring often, for 10 minutes.

Maple syrup is an excellent sweetener for lemonade and cocktails. For an easy, herbal refreshment in the summertime, combine the juice of 2 lemons and 1 orange in a large Mason jar along with your favorite fresh herbs, such as rosemary, mint, basil, thyme, or lemon verbena. Add ¼ cup maple syrup and a pinch of kosher salt and fill the jar with water. Put the lid on and give it a good shake. Store in the refrigerator until you're ready to strain out the solids and pour the liquid into a glass full of ice. Feel free to add your favorite spirit, a fresh herb sprig for a garnish, and a paper straw, of course.

measurement conversions

VOLUME EQUIVALENTS (LIQUID)

US STANDARD	US STANDARD (OUNCES)	METRIC (APPROXIMATE)
2 tablespoons	1 fl. oz.	30 mL
¼ cup	2 fl. oz.	60 mL
½ cup	4 fl. oz.	120 mL
1 cup	8 fl. oz.	240 mL
1½ cups	12 fl. oz.	355 mL
2 cups or 1 pint	16 fl. oz.	475 mL
4 cups or 1 quart	32 fl. oz.	1 L
1 gallon	128 fl. oz.	4 L

OVEN TEMPERATURES

FAHRENHEIT (F)	CELSIUS (C) (APPROXIMATE)
250°F	120°C
300°F	150°C
325°F	165°C
350°F	180°C
375°F	190°C
400°F	200°C
425°F	220°C
450°F	230°C

VOLUME EQUIVALENTS (DRY)

US STANDARD	METRIC (APPROXIMATE)
⅛ teaspoon	0.5 mL
¼ teaspoon	1 mL
½ teaspoon	2 mL
¾ teaspoon	4 mL
1 teaspoon	5 mL
1 tablespoon	15 mL
¼ cup	59 mL
⅓ cup	79 mL
½ cup	118 mL
⅔ cup	156 mL
¾ cup	177 mL
1 cup	235 mL
2 cups or 1 pint	475 mL
3 cups	700 mL
4 cups or 1 quart	1 L

WEIGHT EQUIVALENTS

US STANDARD	METRIC (APPROXIMATE)
½ ounce	15 g
1 ounce	30 g
2 ounces	60 g
4 ounces	115 g
8 ounces	225 g
12 ounces	340 g
16 ounces or 1 pound	455 g

references

Olfert, Melissa D., and Rachel A. Wattick. "Vegetarian Diets and the Risk of Diabetes." *Current Diabetes Reports* 18, no. 11 (2018): 101. DOI.org/10.1007/s11892-018-1070-9.

Sass, Cynthia. "5 Reasons to Try a Vegetarian Diet." *Health.com.* October 8, 2014. ABCNews.go.com/Health/Wellness/reasons-vegetarian-diet/story?id=20473782.

index

about the authors

Husband-and-wife team **Justin Fox Burks** and **Amy Lawrence** are the authors of the cookbooks *The Southern Vegetarian* (2013), *The Chubby Vegetarian* (2016), and *Low-Carb Vegetarian Cookbook* (2020). Currently, they're developing new recipes for their fifth cookbook.

Justin and Amy were invited to cook and to speak at the James Beard Foundation in New York City for the *Enlightened Eaters* series and have appeared on the Food Network's *The Great Food Truck Race* and P. Allen Smith's *Garden Style*. They own Justin Fox Burks Photo Studio in the South Main Arts District in downtown Memphis, Tennessee, and share their inspirations on Instagram (@chubbyveg and @justinfoxburks) and on their blog, The Chubby Vegetarian.

CPSIA information can be obtained
at www.ICGtesting.com
Printed in the USA
JSHW012105120721
16831JS00002B/2